HOW MUCH TO BUY

A Foodservice Purchasing Workbook

Robert A. Ulm

Macmillan Publishing Company
New York

Maxwell Macmillan Canada
Toronto

Maxwell Macmillan International
New York   Oxford   Singapore   Sydney

To Shawn, Shannan, Angela,
Richard, and Sally

Editor: Kevin M. Davis
Production Editor: Jonathan Lawrence
Art Coordinator: Peter A. Robison
Text Designer: Angela Foote
Cover Designer: Cathleen Norz
Production Buyer: Patricia A. Tonneman
Illustrations: Academy ArtWorks, Inc.

This book was set in Century Schoolbook and Frutiger by American-Stratford Graphic Services, Inc., and was printed and bound by Semline, Inc., a Quebecor America Book Group Company. The cover was printed by Phoenix Color Corp.

Macmillan Publishing Company
866 Third Avenue
New York, New York 10022

Macmillan Publishing Company is part of the
Maxwell Communication Group of Companies.

Maxwell Macmillan Canada, Inc.
1200 Eglinton Avenue East, Suite 200
Don Mills, Ontario M3C 3N1

Library of Congress Cataloging-in-Publication Data
Ulm, Robert.
How much to buy : a foodservice purchasing workbook / Robert Ulm.
p. cm.
Includes index.
ISBN 0-02-422101-5
1. Food service—Purchasing. I. Title
TX911.3.P8U46 1994
647.95′068′1—dc20
93-601
CIP

Printing: 1 2 3 4 5 6 7 8 9 Year: 4 5 6 7

Preface

For any product-producing business, it is necessary early on in the business cycle to purchase raw material with which to manufacture the product. In the foodservice business, raw food supplies must be procured, in sufficient quantity, to be available for this manufacture before any food can be prepared for the customer. Since the map, the plan, for the business is the menu, all of the functions carried out in the operation should reflect the business conditions of the menu.

This workbook shows how to purchase for the requirements of a business in the most common menu situations. Each type of operation differs considerably in the way orders are effectively forecasted and put together. For example, purchasing for a restaurant is conducted differently than for an in-plant foodservice, which is, in turn, different from purchasing for a catering operation.

Many purchasing textbooks effectively explain the workings of the market, product identification, and the control aspects of purchasing, and this book is not intended to duplicate this material in any way. Instead, its concern is with how to determine quantities needed and how to physically carry out the act of purchasing. The material answers the question, How much to buy?

Part I of the text discusses menu types, methods of gathering history, and the refined status of food supplies needed. Parts II, III, and IV discuss, respectively, various methods of forecasting, adjustments that need to be made to the forecast, and how to call in an order. Opportunities for practice in calculating these quantities are provided at the ends of individual chapters. The back of the book contains an appendix on measure conversion, a glossary, and answers to the odd-numbered problems.

The main purpose of this workbook is to teach the beginner the basic forecasting techniques that are needed when purchasing for a foodservice. To develop a thorough understanding of these techniques, the student is expected to do the work with a calculator. In the workplace, he or she will undoubtedly encounter some computer work and will have to become computer-literate, but manual calculation of the results will assist in learning these techniques initially.

Many businesses have computer programs that monitor the business and assist the manager. These packages cover all facets of the business in which the manager is involved: general journal, general ledger, payroll, recipes, consumption, history, and forecasts. They can even be set up to keep track of the business of multiple units. Although all major companies have computer programs at the corporate level to assist in these functions, a manager at the unit level may not have these programs available.

Perhaps the most useful arrangement for a foodservice operation is to have a point-of-sale (POS) machine monitoring all front-of-the-house activity, coupled with a back-of-the-house system that controls production functions. The POS machine could provide sales information, while the back-of-the-house computer could assist the manager with such things as usage, inventory, and purchasing material. Both machines, working together, could streamline any managerial effort. As desirable as this is, however, not all cash registers, no matter how sophisticated, can talk to all back-of-the-house computer systems. Also, many businesses don't have these programs because they are very expensive.

The student who takes a position with a foodservice that is using one of these sophisticated systems will have to learn how to use that particular system, but if a job is taken with any number of businesses, one-of-a-kind units, or individual units in a chain, he or she will probably have just a computer to use. In the latter case, managers who wish to streamline their purchasing will probably have to do so themselves, and this is accomplished with a spreadsheet program.

To guide the student in learning how to use spreadsheets, a simple spreadsheet has been selected for use in this workbook. Any spreadsheet the student is using on the job will be able to perform the operations shown. The workbook shows the completed spreadsheet for the student to study, and then explains what formulas were used and how they were placed to obtain the desired results. It is suggested that the student use the computer applications to solve at least one of the problems in each chapter.

Acknowledgments

I would like to express my appreciation to Dennis S. Farley, Central Michigan University; William Jaffe, Purdue University; James R. McClain, California State Polytechnic University–Pomona; Thomas P. Phillips, University of Wisconsin–Stout; W. H. Samenfink, Washington State University; and F. H. Waskey, University of Houston, all of whom reviewed and commented on the manuscript.

I would especially like to thank Professor William Day and Bonnie Ulm for their ideas, and Ruth and Reign Ulm for their help and steadfast support.

Robert A. Ulm

Contents

PART I Foundations

Chapter 1 Menu Types

OVERVIEW

Almost every function in a foodservice is governed by the menu, and purchasing is no exception. Food is purchased for different menus in different ways. From a purchasing point of view, there are three basic types of menus:

1. Sales menus, often called static menus, which remain virtually the same from day to day.
2. Cycle menus, which change every day but repeat when the last menu in the series has been used. Cycle menus are of two types:
   a. equal in length to the number of days they are to cover (e.g., a twenty-menu cycle that covers four five-day weeks); or
   b. longer than the number of days they are to cover (e.g., a twenty-three-menu cycle that covers twenty days), this results in the menus landing on different days each time through the cycle.
3. Special event menus used in catering operations.

Just as each menu has its own characteristics, the best method of purchasing is different for each.

KEY TERMS

Bill of fare

Cycle menu

Equal cycle menu

Long cycle menu

Sales menu

Special event menu

Types of Menus

The first step in any purchasing decision is to identify the needs of the existing menu. The menu largely defines the business, and the method of forecasting one chooses depends on the menu as well. It is the menu that dictates what is to be produced and when, and the purchasing function must support this so that there are always raw materials available, in sufficient quantities, for the production staff to do their job.

There are many different kinds of menus—coffee shop menus, cycle menus, children's menus, special event menus, à la carte menus, and table d'hôte menus, to name but a few—but for forecasting purposes they can be consolidated into three categories:

1. **Sales menu.** This is a menu that is handed to a guest in a restaurant. It can be à la carte or table d'hôte; breakfast or children's. Its major forecasting characteristic is that it usually doesn't change from day to day. Daily specials may change, but the rest of the menu doesn't. This may lead to some boredom in the frequent customer, but it allows the restaurant to specialize in some things and to do often what it does best. The sales menu not only serves as a communication tool by which management can show the guest what the operation offers for service, but ideally will harmonize with the ambience of the business and establish the atmosphere and tone of the foodservice.

2. **Cycle menu.** This menu changes every day and only repeats when the last menu in the list has been used. A cycle menu is useful when one wants a reliable record of historic usage but is likely to find regular returning guests getting bored with the same offerings day after day. To alleviate this possibility, a different menu is used each day but the menus repeat in a cyclical fashion.

   This type of menu is usually used when the business has a somewhat captive audience, such as in-plant, extended care, school lunch, college dormitory, institutional, or even in-flight foodservices. Even commercial airlines tend to feed the same people time after time. Cycle menus have the advantage of repeating menu items in the same combinations when the cycle repeats. This is essential for getting reliable usage information. For example, if a menu contains roast beef and spaghetti, that night's roast beef usage will not provide reliable information on beef usage when roast beef is served with liver and onions rather than spaghetti.

   There are two types of cycle menus that the purchaser should be aware of:

   a. The first is an **equal cycle menu,** one that has as many menus as the number of days the cycle is designed to cover. For example, it may offer twenty-eight menus in a four-week, twenty-eight-day period. Each menu will repeat on the same day of the week each time through the cycle. In other words, if the first menu offers fried chicken, macaroni and cheese, and corned beef and cabbage on the first Monday the cycle is used, that same menu will also appear on the fifth Monday. Because menus repeat on the same day of the week, it is not hard for guests to catch on to the cycle. It may seem unimportant to worry whether the guest will know what is coming up, but in many situations where cycle menus are used boredom is a big factor (after all, a cycle is probably being used to guard against repeat customer boredom in the first place).

   b. The second and more highly recommended type of cycle menu is the **long cycle menu,** one that contains more menus than the number of

GOURMET BURGERS

Our Burgers are made from only the finest fresh ground beef steak, served on a toasted bun. Every burger comes with french fries. All Burgers cooked medium unless otherwise specified.

BURGER–BURGER 8 oz. 4.00
With red onion, tomato, and lettuce.

MUSHROOM & SWISS BURGER 4.75
Topped with big eye Swiss cheese and fresh sauteed mushrooms.

BACON SHROOM CHEESEBURGER . .4.75
Topped with mushrooms, bacon and cheese.

BACON CHEESEBURGER 4.75
With melted Old English Cheese and crisp bacon strips.

OLD ENGLISH CHEESEBURGER 4.50
Covered with double Old English Cheese, red onion, tomato, and lettuce.

PATTIE MELT 4.50
With grilled onions and cheese. Served on rye bread.

DELUXE SANDWICHES

(Not available on Friday & Saturday after 8 p.m.)

FRENCH DIP 4.95
Sliced roast beef on French roll with au jus.

CHICKEN CLUB 4.75
Chicken breast topped with bacon, american cheese, lettuce & tomato. Served on a toasted bun.

BARBECUE BEEF 4.50
Sliced beef with tangy B-B-Q sauce on toasted bun.

CHICKEN CRAB 4.75
Char-broiled chicken breast on a bun, topped with crabmeat and garnished with fresh fruit.

HOT ITALIAN SUB 4.95
Sliced Italian cuts, topped with provolone cheese on a sub roll.

TUNA OR CRAB MELT 5.25
Your choice of tuna or crab salad on pita bread topped with mushrooms and provolone cheese.

HAM AND CHEESE CLUB 4.50
Ham, cheese, lettuce, tomato and mayonnaise.

SALADS

ANTIPASTA SALAD 4.95
Chilled romaine topped with Italian meats and cheese, olives, tomatoes, eggs, artichoke hearts, red and green bell peppers, with house dressing.

CRAB LOUIE 5.95
A special salad topped with avocados, crabmeat, tomato, sliced eggs, and garnished with fresh fruit of the season.

MISS JULIE-ANN 4.75
Select salad greens, turkey, ham, cheddar, and swiss cheese, avocado, tomatoes, egg, and garnished with fresh fruit of the season.

SPINACH SALAD 4.95
Fresh spinach topped with procuitto ham, mushrooms, eggs and tomatoes. Served with bacon dressing.

SHRIMP SALAD 5.95
Shrimps swimming in lettuce, hard-boiled egg, cheddar and swiss cheese, tomatoes, cucumbers, artichoke heart, olives, garnished with fruit of the season.

VILLAGE SALAD 4.95
Tomatoes, cucumbers, romaine, greek cheese, olives, green peppers, anchovies, onions and herbs. (Pappas Famous Greek Salad Also Available)

CEASARS SALAD 4.75
Chilled romaine lettuce, served with homemade croutons, anchovies, grated parmesan cheese and our special dressing.

FOR OUR YOUNGER FRIENDS

Served with Soft Drink or Milk

SPAGHETTI .2.95
With meat sauce.

FRIED 1/4 CHICKEN 3.25
With French fries.

HAMBURGER 2.95
With French fried potatoes.

FRENCH FRIED SHRIMP 4.25
With French fries.

LAKE PERCH 4.25
Fried, served with French fried potatoes.

B-B-Q RIBS .3.95
With French fried potatoes.

OLD TIME FAVORITES

Served with soup or tomato juice, salad or cottage cheese, choice of baked, cottage fries, french fries, rice or pasta.

BROASTED CHICKEN 6.95
A half chicken with broasted potato wedges.

IRON RICH PAN FRIED LIVER 6.95
Sauteed onions and bacon.

BREADED PORK TENDERLOIN 6.95
With spaghetti or Fettuccine.

CHOP SIRLOIN 6.95
Over 10 ozs. of ground sirloin topped with grilled onions and au jus.

B-B-Q RIBS . . . . 1/2 Slab – 6.95
. . . . Full Slab – 10.95

B-B-Q CHICKEN 7.25
1/2 B-B-Q chicken with hickory barbecue sauce.

ROASTED CHICKEN OREGANO 7.25
Slowly roasted chicken with a delicate blend of seasonings.

STEAK AND SHRIMP 14.95
8 oz. filet mignon accompanied with four fried shrimp.

CHICKEN AND RIBS COMBO 8.75
The best of both, 1/2 slab of our delicious ribs and 1/4 of a chicken.

DIET PLATES

For The Health Conscious

FILET MIGNON 10.95
8 oz. filet with cottage cheese, fruit and more.

CHICKEN DIET PLATE 8.25
Broiled breast of chicken served with apples, cantaloupe and much more.

ORANGE ROUGHY 8.25
Broiled orange roughy served with fresh vegetables and our tossed salad with tarragon vinegar on the side.

CHICKEN, VEGETABLES & RICE 8.25
Broiled chicken breast served with fresh vegetables and rice.

BROILED SHRIMP & VEGETABLES . .10.25
Gulf shrimp broiled and served with fresh vegetables and rice.

CHOPPED SIRLOIN 7.75
8 oz. ground sirloin served with cottage cheese and fresh fruit.

POACHED SALMON 10.95
Fresh salmon poached. Served with fresh vegetables and our tossed salad with tarragon vinegar on the side.

**BROILED LAKE PERCH,
VEGETABLES AND RICE** 9.95
Delicate fresh water perch broiled. Served with fresh vegetables and our tossed salad with tarragon vinegar on the side.

STEAMED VEGETABLES 7.25
Assorted fresh vegetables.

SUNSET SPECIALS

Served with soup or salad, choice of baked potato, cottage fries, French fries, rice or pasta.

Monday - Friday 4 - 6 pm   •   Saturday & Sunday 12 - 4 pm

LAKE PERCH 5.95		**LIVER & ONIONS** 5.95
BROASTED CHICKEN 5.95		**B.B.Q. CHICKEN** 5.95
CHOP SIRLOIN 5.95		**ORANGE ROUGHY** 5.95
CHICKEN PICCATTA 5.95		**CATFISH** 5.95
FETTUCCINE ALFREDO 4.25		**1/2 SLAB RIBS** 5.95
LASAGNA 5.95		**CHEESE OR MEAT RAVIOLI** 5.95
SPAGHETTI 5.95		

Sales Menu

Dinner -- Day 12 through 18 of 34 -- Spring / Summer Cycle

Course	Monday	Rec#	Tuesday	Rec#	Wednesday	Rec#	Thursday	Rec#	Friday	Rec#	Saturday	Rec#	Sunday	Rec
Soup	Vegetabl	A 18	ChixNood	A 12	Fr Onion	A 16	BBouillo	A 79	Tomato	A 8	Egg Drop	A 28	BfBarle	A 35
	Potato	A 68	Broccoli	A 82	Cauliflow	A 31	NavyBean	A 83	CanaChez	A 46	SplitPea	A 97	ChGumbo	A 71
Entree	BBQ Ribs	P 37	Rst Beef	B 52	FF Chix	B 52	PorkChop	F 12	Bkd Ham	P 93	CornBeef	B 64	ChixKie	F 76
	FFShrimp	E 22	Spaghett	B 4	Chow Mein	B 4	ChpSteak	P 42	TurkDres	B 11	PorkFrRi	P 127	PSausag	P 98
	ChiliMac	P 40	TurkPotP	F 36	Meatloaf	F 36	ChixTaco	B 76	Bkd Ziti	F 31	SwMeatbs	B 73	BStroga	B 44
	DenOmlet	C 72	Bkd Cod	E 31	BkdSalmon	E 31	ChezSouf	E 90	SoleAlmo	C 52	StfdFlou	E 59	ShmpNew	E 3
Veg.	Cut Corn	V 27	GrnBeans	V 12	Peas&Mush	V141	Broccoli	V 21	Zucchini	V 14	Cabbage	V 31	WintMix	V 99
	BrusSpts	V 36	Cauliflo	V 29	SlCarrots	V 62	Mxd Veg	V 19	BrTomato	V 61	Spinach	V100	Sauerkr	V 74
	StwdToma	V 47	Bu Beets	V 73	Turnips	V 55	Ratatoul	V 88	FrCutBea	V 57	Pea&Carr	V 66	FavaBea	V 27
Starch	MshdPota	V 93	MshdPota	V 93	MshdPotat	V 93	MshdPota	V 93	MshdPota	V 93	MshdPota	V 93	MshdPot	V 93
	BkdBeans	V 52	Brn Rice	V 87	Wht Rice	V 36	Frijoles	V 54	CandYam	V 62	ParBuPot	V 9	WhtRice	V 36
Salads	Tossed	S 1	Tossed	S 1	Tossed	S 1	Tossed	S 1	Tossed	S 1	Tossed	S 1	Tossed	S 1
	ColeSlaw	S 35	3 Bean	S 62	Tom&Peppe	S 62	KidneyBe	S 41	RelishPl	S 48	StfdCele	S 89	Cuke&Cr	S 99
	CottChez	S 3	PotSalad	S 75	MacSalad	S 75	Car/Rais	S121	PastaSal	S113	GerPotSa	S 22	MarArti	S 65
	FruitJel	S 16	FruitJel	S 16	FruitJel	S 16	FruitJel	S 16	FruitJel	S 16	FruitJel	S 16	FruitJe	S 16
	CitrusSa	S137	Waldorf	S 47	BananaNut	S 47	BlshPear	S 86	SpiPeach	S 22	FrosGrap	S 81	Ambrosi	S 72
Desert	GerChoCa	D 63	YellowCa	D 51	AngelCake	D 51	WhiteCak	D 13	MarbleCa	D 96	WalnutCa	D 47	RaspTor	D 11
	CherryPi	D 9	ApplePie	D 93	PeachPie	D 93	BBerryPi	D 34	StberryP	D 72	MinceMPi	D 17	PecanPi	D 2
	LemCrPie	D 29	BanCrPie	D 28	KeyLimePi	D 28	CustardP	D 86	BosCrPie	D 39	ButschPi	D 50	ChoCrPi	D 63
	AstFrFru		AstFrFru		AstFrFrui		AstFrFru		AstFrFru		AstFrFru		AstFrFru	
	Jel/Pud		Jel/Pud		Jel/Pudd		Jel/Pud		Jel/Pud		Jel/Pud		Jel/Pud	
Grill	BBQ Beef	B 54	MbalSand	B 24	PoSausage	P 19	ChiliDog	P 19	ItalBeef	B 20	FF Clams	E 13	Burrito	V 46
	Hamburg	B 17	Hamburg	B 17	Hamburg	B 17	Hamburg	B 17	Hamburg	B 17	Hamburg	B 17	Hamburg	B 17
	Hot Dog	B 23	Hot Dog	B 23	Hot Dog	B 23	Hot Dog	B 23	Hot Dog	B 23	Hot Dog	B 23	Hot Dog	B 23
	GrilChez	C 11	GrilChez	C 11	GrilCheez	C 11	GrilChez	C 11	GrilChez	C 11	GrilChez	C 11	GrlChez	C 11
	Ham&Chez	P 74	Ham&Chez	P 74	Ham&Chez	P 74	Ham&Chez	P 74	Ham&Chez	P 74	Ham&Chez	P 74	Hm&Chez	P 74
	Fish&Chp	E 41	Fish&Chp	E 41	Fish&Chp	E 41	Fish&Chp	E 41	Fish&Chp	E 41	Fish&Chp	E 41	Fsh&Chp	E 41
	ISausage	P 39	ISausage	P 39	ItSausage	P 39	ISausage	P 39	ISausage	P 39	ISausage	P 39	ISausag	P 39
	Submarin	B 96	Submarin	B 96	Submarine	B 96	Submarin	B 96	Submarin	B 96	Submarin	B 96	Submari	B 96
	F Fries	V 32	F Fries	V 32	F Fries	V 32	F Fries	V 32	F Fries	V 32	F Fries	V 32	F Fries	V 32
	OnionRng	V 58	OnionRng	V 58	OnionRng	V 58	OnionRng	V 58	OnionRng	V 58	OnionRng	V 58	OnionRg	V 58
	HushPupp	V 47	HushPupp	V 47	HushPuppy	V 47	HushPupp	V 47	HushPupp	V 47	HushPupp	V 47	HushPup	V 47

Cycle Menu

days in the cycle. For example, thirty-one different menus may be used to cover a twenty-eight-day, four-week period. This way menus don't repeat on the same day of the week, since the first menu will skip three weekdays before it repeats (i.e., if the cycle started on a Monday, it will begin the second time through on a Thursday). This characteristic has two advantages. First, the forecaster still has the advantage of the reliable historic records that can be generated from a cycle menu; and second, future menus do not repeat on the same day of the week, making the cycle harder to predict and giving the guest less opportunity to be bored. This type of cycle is highly recommended for many foodservices.

3. **Special event menu.** This menu is formulated for one event and may never be used again. Special event menus are used in all kinds of catering applications and for special holiday offerings in other operations as well.

Many operations may use all three menu types. An in-plant operation will probably have an unchanging sales menu for its breakfast and grill operation, a cycle menu for its lunches and dinners, and will often serve special parties when needed. Forecasts of food needs for such a foodservice would need to take into consideration the requirements of all three menu types.

Special Event Menu

One other term should be mentioned here. A **bill of fare** is a list of items offered by the business. Unlike a sales menu, which usually includes item descriptions and a high degree of marketing, the bill of fare is simply the unadorned list of what the foodservice offers to its guests, as is often found in a fast-food or deli operation. It may take an artist, a writer, and a printer to make a sales menu, but the management alone formulates the bill of fare.

SANDWICHES	SALADS	BEVERAGES
Served on Rye, whiTe,	Chef 3.59	Pepsi, DieT Pepsi, Dr Pepper,
kaiser Roll, PiTa PockeT,	Grilled Chicken ... 3.59	Caffeine Free DieT Pepsi,
WheaT, or Bagel	Tuna 3.59	RooTbeer, MT. Dew ..... .79
Corned Beef 3.39	Chicken 3.59	Iced Tea .... .79
PasTrami 3.39	PasTa 2.69	Coffee sm. .65 lg. .85
Sandwiches lisTed below	Garden 1.69	HoT Tea .... .65
include leTTuce and TomaTo	Cole Slaw ...... .99	FruiT Drinks .... .99
RoasT Beef 3.39	PoTaTo Salad ..... .99	Milk .... .95
Turkey 3.19	Dressings: Creamy	HoT ChocolaTe ...... .85
Ham 3.19	ITalian, LiTe ITalian,	Cup of Ice .... .10
Salami 3.19	1000 Island, French,	Sparklers 1.29
BLT 3.19	Ranch, LiTe Ranch	Soup Du Jour .... Bowl 1.89
Tuna Salad 3.39	BAGELS	Cup 1.49
Chicken Salad 3.39	Bagel & BuTTer .... .75	Brownie .... .85
Egg Salad 2.69	Bagel & Jelly .... .85	
Cheese 2.69	Bagel & BuTTer & Jelly ...... .95	
EXTRAS	Bagel & Cream Cheese 1.19	
Cheese: American, Swiss,	Bagel & Cream Cheese & Jelly ... 1.45	
Colby, or Mozzarella ..49	Bagel – Plain .... .59	
Cream Cheese ...... .50	PeanuT BuTTer add .... .50	
	ExTra Cream Cheese ...... .35	

Bill of Fare

Chapter 2 Gathering History

To best predict what will happen in the future, it is often best to begin with what happened in the past. This holds true for purchasing for foodservices. History is usually collected in two ways: by recording what was sold in the dining room and by keeping track of food exiting the kitchen. A menu scatter sheet reflects dining room sales, and ably supports a sales menu: a food production sheet records food leaving the kitchen, and is a fine tool for any menu situation.

KEY TERMS

Customer count

Food production sheet

Menu scatter sheet

History Gathering

It's easier to know what to expect in the future if one has a clear understanding of what happened in the past, so the best foundation on which to build expectations of future needs is history. Even though many operations keep little or no sales or production history, it makes sense to do so. This is particularly true in regard to purchasing. The menu shows what foods were served, but the **customer count** (number of customers served) and the amount of food they consumed is equally important.

There are two common ways of recording history: keeping track of how much food is sold in the dining room, or recording how much food leaves the kitchen (i.e., record sales or keep track of production). These are not newly invented techniques, but tried and true ways of collecting history. There are

9

certain advantages to each method, but both provide a useful and accurate look at history.

Menu Scatter Sheet

On page 11 is an example of a **menu scatter sheet.** Depending on the establishment, data are presented in different ways, but most yield the same type of information. Originally this report was prepared by the cashier or hostess from guest checks, but now it's usually prepared automatically by preset electronic cash registers. The menu scatter sheet has the following features:

1. It is a sales document, a record of food sold. It is a dining room record and is compiled from guest checks or a preset cash register.
2. It tells how many of each menu item were sold in a particular time period (e.g., a meal, a day, or a week).
3. It indicates the revenue contributed by a particular menu item for that time period.
4. It gives the percentage of total net revenue obtained from the sales of each menu item. (The percent contribution to sales is often used for purposes beyond the scope of this book.)
5. Other information, such as customer count, weather conditions, or special events should also be included on the scatter sheet. Mention of these factors is necessary because they will affect usage and therefore will influence percent contribution to sales somewhat from one week to the next.

As can be seen from the form, the number of each menu item sold is first tallied and then totaled. Then the revenue contributed by the item is calculated, and finally its percent contribution to sales is recorded as a percent of total business net sales. A menu scatter sheet is usually used for a week's business activity, but can be used for any period desired.

Food Production Sheet

The **food production sheet** is a record of food that has been prepared and then used in one of several ways. It shows how much food has left the kitchen at the end of a meal. An example of a food production sheet is on page 12. As with a menu scatter sheet, the food production sheet can appear in many different forms, but it usually has the following features:

1. It is often used as a production order form. The manager or executive chef will fill in the "amount to prepare" column so that the cooking or pantry staff knows how much to produce.
2. Sometimes the cook does not, or possibly cannot, prepare the amount specified. For example, if the cook is told to make 300 servings of chili and has only enough ground beef for 100 servings, the record should say that only 100 servings were produced, not 300.
3. At the end of a meal period, the amount of food left over is recorded. Both the amount with which one started and the amount left over are necessary to figure out how much was used. If the food ran out too soon, this column shouldn't be left blank. It would be misleading to make no comment about a run-out because it will look like the item lasted and ran out at the very end of the meal.

There are two common ways to record a run-out: The best way is to indicate how many customers had been *served* at the time the food item ran out (CC RO). For example, if 400 people were served when the entrée was used up, and if 500 people were served for the entire meal, the item

Menu Scatter Sheet

Menu Item	Guest Check Sales Tally							Total Sold	×	Selling Price	=	Menu Item Revenue Contribution	÷	Total Net Sales	=	Percent Contribution to Sales
	M	T	W	T	F	S	S									
									×		=		÷		=	
									×		=		÷		=	
									×		=		÷		=	
									×		=		÷		=	
									×		=		÷		=	
									×		=		÷		=	
									×		=		÷		=	
									×		=		÷		=	
									×		=		÷		=	
									×		=		÷		=	
									×		=		÷		=	
									×		=		÷		=	
									×		=		÷		=	
									×		=		÷		=	
									×		=		÷		=	

Customer Count:

Comments:

Food Production Sheet   Day: _____   Date ___/___/___

Customer Count: _____

Menu Item	Portion Size	Amount to Prepare	Amount Actually Prepared	Amount Left Over or CC RO or Time RO	Amount Used

Comments:

12

lasted through 80 percent of the meal. The simplest way to record a run-out is by the *time* that the food item ran out (Time RO). For example, a notation that an entrée ran out at 6:00 P.M., when the meal period lasted until 7:00 P.M., will assist the planner more than simply saying that none of the entrée was left over.

4. The "amount used" column is the major reason for filling out the form. Subtracting the amount of food left over from the amount actually produced yields the quantity of food actually used. Actually, it is not necessarily food used but the amount of food that has exited the kitchen. This food may not have been used in the way hoped (sold to customers), but it is nonetheless gone. Ready-to-serve food, not raw ingredients can usually leave the kitchen in three ways:

   a. *Sales:* most of the food that leaves the kitchen will be sold.

   b. *Employee meals:* employees may or may not be supplied food, but if they are this is a legitimate path for food to leave the kitchen.

   c. *Waste:* this is an unplanned exit from the kitchen. This type of waste has several forms: overportioning, overcooking, spillage, and theft (not from the storeroom, because that kind of theft will happen before the food ever appears on the production sheet: this would be theft of the final product, such as an employee giving food to friends).

   The production sheet does not tell a manager which of these three ways the food was used. It just tells how much food left the kitchen. If the food ran out early, the manager might put an estimate in the "amount used" column of how much would have been needed. When an item runs out, however, the forecaster must remember that a run-out of one item, particularly a popular item, will probably cause an unnatural increase in sales of the remaining menu items.

5. This form may also provide space for comments regarding weather, customer count, and other information that may have a bearing on usage.

Using the Sheets Effectively

On pages 14 and 15 are filled-out examples of the two sheets just as discussed. Study them to see what happened during those meals. The tally marks on the menu scatter sheet were made from guest checks, rather than taken from a preset cash register, which is much faster and more accurate. These examples include only entrées, but one could do a scatter sheet for the entire menu (although it's most important to watch high cost items). Note that the amount used on the food production sheet for Saturday is at least as much as the amount shown as sold on the Saturday scatter sheet.

Most food usage history can be kept on one of these two records. Which one is selected may depend on what type of menu is being used. Almost any kind of foodservice, using any type of menu, can easily record its history on a food production sheet; this sheet could even be used as a fill sheet for a vending operation. A scatter sheet, on the other hand, is easiest to use when there is a preset cash register or when guest checks are readily available. Thus, a scatter sheet is best used in an operation that utilizes a regular sales menu, and a food production sheet is preferred when a foodservice is using a cycle menu or in a catering situation.

A restaurant could use *both* types of record keeping, although few actually do so, and many probably don't keep usage records at all. In a regular restaurant it is sensible to keep both types of history in case the business gets off track, or simply to ensure that it will stay on track. And any foodservice can benefit from an accurate history of usage.

Menu Scatter Sheet

Menu Item	Guest Check Sales Tally							Total Sold	×	Selling Price	=	Menu Item Revenue Contribution	÷	Total Net Sales	=	Percent Contribution to Sales
	M	T	W	T	F	S	S									
Fried chicken								99	×	$8.50	=	$841.50	÷	$18,342.21	=	4.6%
Pot roast								60	×	$11.95	=	$717.00	÷	$18,342.21	=	3.9%
Pork chops								56	×	$9.50	=	$532.00	÷	$18,342.21	=	2.9%
Corned beef								63	×	$8.75	=	$551.25	÷	$18,342.21	=	3.0%
Roast turkey								68	×	$10.25	=	$697.00	÷	$18,342.21	=	3.8%
New York strip steak								140	×	$13.75	=	$1,925.00	÷	$18,342.21	=	10.5%
Filet mignon								128	×	$11.50	=	$1,472.00	÷	$18,342.21	=	8.0%
Chicken kiev								101	×	$10.95	=	$1,105.95	÷	$18,342.21	=	6.0%
								757								
Customer Count:	56	67	68	98	129	177	162									

Comments: Rainy Monday

No special parties all week

14

Food Production Sheet   Day: Saturday   Date: 7 / 11 / 92

Customer Count: 177

Menu Item	Portion Size	Amount to Prepare	Amount Actually Prepared	Amount Left Over or CC RO or Time RO	Amount Used
Fried chicken	1/2 Chix	35 S	34 S	8 S	26 S
Pot roast 30% W	7 oz AS	Roast 13 lb AP	13 lb AP	RO 7:30 8:00 end	14 lb AP would last
Pork chops	2-5 oz	30 chops	32 chops	2 chops	30 chops
Corned beef 50% W	7 oz AS	Boil 14 lb AP	16 lb AP	102 of 164 cust.	25 lb AP would last
Roast turkey 42% W	7 oz AS	Roast 16 lb AP	15 lb AP	1 lb EP	13.3 lb AP
New York strip steak	14 oz AP	33 each	29 each	4 each raw	29 each
Filet mignon	8 oz AP	35 each	30 each	5 each raw	30 each
Chicken kiev	8 oz AP	as needed	18 each	0 left	18 each

Comments: Portion and thaw the above. Cook and portion insides, brisket, and turkey breast. Cook chicken and chops half way,

finish to order. Cook steaks and kievs to order only.

Chapter 3 State of Refinement

OVERVIEW

Food undergoes continual refinement from its raw state at the time of purchase to its final form as a finished product, consumed by the guest. When discussing quantities, it is important that the purchasing agent understand each stage of production. Each state becomes progressively smaller as the food becomes further refined, and each stage implies its own waste factor as the raw material is trimmed, cooked, and portioned away. All food begins AP, "as purchased." As it is refined into the finished product, it becomes ready to serve and is referred to as AS, "as served." Finally the customer consumes it, and this quantity is called EP, "edible portion." If the purchasing agent keeps each of these concepts in mind, he or she will be able to buy the correct quantity of food.

KEY TERMS

AS—as served

AP—as purchased

EP—edible portion

W—waste

W%—waste percentage

State of Refinement

When referring to a quantity of food, it is essential to be clear on its state of refinement. Is it raw? Is it cleaned? Is it trimmed? Each state of refinement has its inherent trim or loss waste that has to be accounted for when preparing or purchasing that food. For the following discussion, keep in mind these definitions:

AP: as purchased. AP is the purchased amount, the amount of raw material one begins with in preparing the dish. It is the total. It is 100%, the raw amount received on the dock.

AS: as served. AS is the more refined amount that will be served to the customer. It will usually be smaller than AP because of cleaning, trimming, cooking, and portioning losses.

EP: edible portion. EP is the amount of food the customer is expected to eat. It is smaller than AS because of inedible parts such as seeds, bones, and fat.

W: waste. W is the amount of AP lost to obtain AS or EP. Waste is *always* some part of AP. AS and EP have already had the waste removed.

W%: waste percentage. W% is the amount of waste expressed as a percentage of AP: $W\% = (W/AP) \times 100$.

The various states of a T-bone steak can be used to illustrate AS, AP, and EP:

AP: 16 oz—raw, just as it was received.
AS: 12 oz—trimmed and cooked, serving given to guest.
EP: 9 oz—meat eaten by the customer, with bone and
                      some fat left on the plate.

Many times these concepts will overlap. If whole apples are served, AP and AS will be the same. If fruit cocktail is served, AS and EP will be the same. For a candy bar, AP, AS, and EP will all be the same.

These concepts must be kept in mind when ordering, or the wrong amount might be purchased. For instance, if 2 lb of pulled, cooked meat are needed for a chicken salad recipe, don't try to get by with a raw 2-lb chicken. From a whole, raw bird to cooked, pulled meat up to 50% can be lost in bone, skin, trim, and cooking loss. So, begin with at least a 4-lb, whole, raw chicken to end up with 2 lb of meat ready for the salad. In other words, purchase 4 lb of AP chicken to get 2 lb of AS meat.

These refining concepts are related mathematically:

$$AP = AS + W \quad \text{or}$$
$$AS = AP - W \quad \text{or}$$
$$W = AP - AS$$

Go over these three equations to form a clear mental picture of their relationships. Remember, W is always some part of AP, not AS, and AP is 100%.

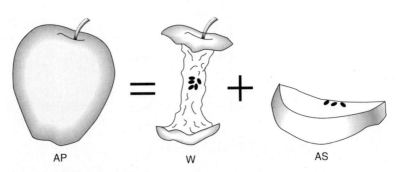

AP   W   AS

As Purchased to As Served

OVERVIEW

By building on an understanding of the concept of yield, or the various states of refinement that food undergoes, a technique can be developed for calculating how much raw food is required to provide the needed amount of cooked, portioned food. With this AS to AP conversion formula, one can forecast the needs of the expected guests and calculate how much raw food should be purchased to feed them the proper amount of cooked food.

KEY TERM

AS/AP formula

AS to AP Conversion

When trying to figure out how much to buy for a party, begin by calculating AS. This is done in a number of ways, but it's often determined by multiplying expected customer count by the portion size. AS is usually an easy quantity to estimate. For example, if 700 people are expected at a party and each is to receive a 3-oz AS portion, the total AS is 131.25 lb:

$$700 \text{ cust.} \times \frac{3 \text{ oz}}{\text{cust.}} \times \frac{1 \text{ lb}}{16 \text{ oz.}} = 131.25 \text{ lb AS}$$

After estimating how much AS is needed, the next thing to figure out is how much AP must be purchased so that there will be enough AP to trim, cook, and portion and still end up with enough AS to serve the guests. To get from AS to AP, it is helpful to know what percentage of AP is likely to be lost as the product is refined to AS. Waste percentage (W%) will always be treated as a part of AP. Waste percentages of many raw foods can be found in food purchasing books, but are best determined by personal experience. To determine a product's waste percentage experimentally, do an experiment like the following:

1. Weigh the raw, unrefined product you are working with to determine the weight of AP.
2. Refine the item to its cooked, portioned state and get the weight of AS. The difference between the AP weight of the product and its AS weight will be the waste (W) weight.
3. Divide W by the AP weight, the total, and multiply your answer by 100, and you will have a real waste percentage for that product.

It isn't necessary to repeat this operation every time the product is served but it is advisable to check the results periodically to maintain a realistic W% for that commodity. Then the number can be used in all future calculations dealing with that food. (*Note:* this workbook contains many waste percentages that the author has made up to illustrate the mathematical concepts presented. These should not be used for actual purchasing on the job. The best way to get an accurate waste percentage is to conduct one's own yield test.)

If AS and W% are known, the AP amount can be calculated. Here is some algebra that will help to determine AP, given AS and W%. Begin with the following equation:

$$\frac{\text{AP weight}}{\text{AP\%}} = \frac{\text{AS weight}}{\text{AS\%}}$$

This can be simplified by dividing both sides of the equation by the label "weight":

$$\frac{\text{AP weight}}{\text{AP\%} \times \text{weight}} = \frac{\text{AS weight}}{\text{AS\%} \times \text{weight}}$$

so that the equation becomes

$$\frac{\text{AP}}{\text{AP\%}} = \frac{\text{AS}}{\text{AS\%}}$$

Now remember that AS% = AP% − W% and AP% = 100%, so

$$\frac{\text{AP}}{100\%} = \frac{\text{AS}}{\text{AP\%} - \text{W\%}}$$

To isolate AP, multiply both sides of the equation by 100%:

$$100\% \times \frac{\text{AP}}{100\%} = \frac{\text{AS}}{\text{AP\%} - \text{W\%}} \times 100\%$$

This yields

$$\text{AP} = \frac{\text{AS} \times 100\%}{\text{AP\%} - \text{W\%}}$$

And since AP% is 100%, the equation becomes

$$\text{AP} = \frac{\text{AS} \times 100\%}{100\% - \text{W\%}}$$

Because of the minus sign in the denominator, the 100%s can't be canceled. But because of that same minus sign, the % signs can be canceled, so the finished formula looks like this:

$$\text{AP} = \frac{\text{AS} \times 100}{100 - \text{W}}$$

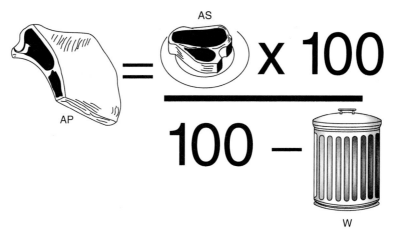

The AS/AP Formula

In this workbook, this formula will be referred to as the yield formula or the **AS/AP formula**.

Here's why this yield formula is such a fine tool:

1. The amount of AS needed for an occasion can usually be estimated.
2. The waste percentages of commonly used items are not difficult to find.
3. This method is very accurate.
4. It's quick. Once AS is known, it can be multiplied by 100 mentally by the addition of two zeros. That will consolidate the numerator. The denominator can usually be determined mentally also. So the formula really becomes one division problem with a calculator.

Think of this formula as an equation that has two pigeon holes:

$$AP = \frac{AS \times 100}{100 - W}$$

When using it, plug in the weight (or volume) of the AS that is needed into the AS pigeon hole. Then plug in the W% (as a whole number) of that commodity into the waste pigeon hole. Now AP will be given in the same units that were used for AS.

▓▓▓▓▓ EXAMPLE

You are going to feed 200 people 4 oz of cooked inside round each. How much should you buy in its raw state? Insides shrink about 30% to trimming, cooking, and portioning.

Solution

To solve this problem, first calculate the AS amount needed:

$$200 \text{ people} \times \frac{4 \text{ oz}}{\text{person}} \times \frac{1 \text{ lb}}{16 \text{ oz}} = \frac{200 \times 4 \text{ lb}}{16} = 50 \text{ lb AS}$$

Now plug this AS amount and the W% for insides into the AS/AP formula:

$$\frac{50 \text{ lb} \times 100}{100 - 30} = \frac{5000 \text{ lb}}{70} = 71.429 \text{ lb or about 72 lb AP}$$

You should buy at least 72 lb of inside round to feed this party.

Remember not to convert from AS to AP by applying the W% to the AS amount calculated. Waste is a percentage of AP, not AS. The yield formula is the best way to get from AS estimates of need, to how much to buy in AP terms.

In this workbook, use the yield formula whenever some kind of waste is likely to occur. In actual practice, many commodities are not expensive enough to warrant the time spent in calculations. For example, if 35 lb of cooked, sliced carrots are needed, buy a 50-lb sack of them and don't bother with formulas. The AS/AP formula is for keeping major purchasing expenditures in line, not for busy work. However, it is important to use this idea—or some other method that deals with shrinkage—when buying meat, seafood, or other expensive items, because overpurchasing will affect food costs.

▓▓▓▓ EXAMPLE

How many cases of Red Delicious apples will you need if each case weighs 45 lb AP and you plan to give 500 guests 6 oz of AS sliced apples each? You can assume that these apples lose about 26% of their AP weight when they are cored and sliced.

Solution

1. Calculate the AS desired:

$$500 \text{ people} \times \frac{6 \text{ oz}}{\text{person}} \times \frac{1 \text{ lb}}{16 \text{ oz}} = \frac{500 \times 6 \text{ lb}}{16} = 187.500 \text{ lb AS}$$

2. Plug this information into the yield formula:

$$AP = \frac{187.500 \text{ lb} \times 100}{100 - 26} = \frac{18{,}750 \text{ lb}}{74} = 253.378 \text{ lb AP}$$

3. Convert AP pounds to cases of AP apples:

$$253.378 \text{ lb AP} \times \frac{1 \text{ case}}{45 \text{ lb AP}} = 5.631, \text{ or about 6 cases}$$

▓▓▓▓ EXAMPLE

How many pounds of raw corned beef brisket, with the deckle on, should you buy to feed 325 people 3.5 oz of shaved, cooked corn beef? Raw to cooked, shaved corned beef brisket has a waste percentage of 48%.

Solution

1. Calculate the AS needs for this party:

$$325 \text{ people} \times \frac{3.5 \text{ oz}}{\text{person}} \times \frac{1 \text{ lb}}{16 \text{ oz}} = \frac{325 \times 3.5 \text{ lb}}{16} = 71.094 \text{ lb AS}$$

2. Put the information in the yield formula:

$$AP = \frac{71.094 \times 100}{100 - 48} = \frac{7109.4 \text{ lb}}{52} = 136.719 \text{ lb AP}$$

3. Buy about 137 lb of raw corned beef brisket.

Problems

The answers to the odd-numbered problems are given in the back of the book.

1. How much green, headless shrimp must you purchase in order to have 35 lb of cooked, peeled, deveined shrimp for your party? You can figure that the peeling and cooking loss of green shrimp is 37%.

2. If broccoli loses 21% to trim and cooking, and you need to have 48 lb of cooked broccoli, how much fresh broccoli should you buy?

3. If you plan to serve each guest 4.5 oz of London broil, how much raw flank steak should you buy to feed 175 people? Figure that trimming, cooking, and portioning waste is 26%.

4. How many 2½-pound fryers will you need if the party requires 40 lb of cooked, pulled meat and a fryer has a 51% waste factor?

5. What is the waste percentage, to the nearest tenth of a percent, on diced yellow globe onions if you start with 78 lb of whole, unpeeled onions, and end up with 70 lb of diced onions?

6. How many pounds of Thompson seedless grapes will you need if the recipe calls for 35 lb and the stem waste is 8%?

7. How large a steamship round should you get (round your answer up to the nearest 10 lb) if you want to carve 7 oz of cooked round for each of your expected 55 guests? Figure a waste percentage of 46%.

8. How much usable meat is a 28-lb raw turkey likely to yield, if it has a 41% waste factor? How many 3-oz servings will that give you if you have no further losses?

9. Which turkey product will feed your 18 guests 7 oz each, a 13-lb raw, bone-in breast, or a ready-cooked 13-lb boneless breast? The raw breast has an AP to AS loss of 37%, and the cooked breast will lose about 1.5% to warming and the slicer during portioning.

10. If you need 75 lb of cooked, sliced pork loin, which has a shrink of 35%, how much raw BRT pork loin should you buy?

11. For which food will AS and EP be the same? whole apples? mashed potatoes? flame Tokay grapes? a rack of baby back ribs? For which will AP and EP be the same? a T-bone steak? a whole peach? a package of M&M's? a banana?

12. If potatoes lose 13% to peeling and trimming, how many pounds of diced potatoes will you probably get from a 100-lb sack of raw, unpeeled reds?

13. The potato salad recipe calls for 13 lb of peeled, cooked, diced potatoes. To feed your party you'll have to make five recipes. How many pounds of raw reds will you need if they have a waste factor of 13%?

14. If a raw T-bone steak weighs 20 oz, has a 25% cooking loss, and a 43% bone and inedible fat loss, how much will you serve the guest? How much is he or she likely to eat? (Remember, all waste is a percentage of AP.)

15. If a pint of orange juice weighs a pound, how many cases of 88 Temples will you need to squeeze 20 gal of juice? A case of 88 Temples weighs 45 lb and Temples have a whole to juice waste factor of 52%.

16. What is the W% on gooseneck round if you begin with 215 lb AP and end up with exactly 600 3.5-oz servings AS?

17. If you have 35 lb of cooked, sliced outside round on hand, how much raw outside should you buy to have a total of 48 lb of cooked, sliced beef for your sandwich buffet? Outsides have an AP to AS waste of 29%.

18. How much will it cost you to buy enough ham to serve 85 lb of cooked, sliced ham if whole, bone-in hams weigh 18 lb AP, have an AP to AS waste percentage of 44%, and cost $1.83 per AP pound?

19. How many 28-lb cases of Concord grapes will you need to produce four cases of homemade wine? Remember, a bottle is ⅕ of a gallon, there are 12 bottles in a case, a pint of grape juice weighs 1 lb, and Concord grapes have an AP to juice waste of 47%.

20. How many dozen AA large eggs will you need to make an angel cake formula 10 times if the formula calls for 3 lb 7 oz of egg whites? Give your answer in whole dozens. A dozen large eggs weigh 24 oz, and the egg white yield on an egg is 53%.

PART II Forecasts

Chapter **5** *Customer Count*

OVERVIEW

One of the major concerns in any forecast is how many guests will need to be served. By building a forecasted customer count from a historical customer count, the buyer can make a logical and accurate purchase.

Customer Count

Many forecasting procedures utilize a customer count, so keeping historical records of customers is necessary. The customer count may be for whatever time period is relevant (e.g., the meal, the day, or even the week, month, or fiscal year), and is found in various ways depending on the setting: for example, in a restaurant, count the number of guests served, as indicated by the cash register or guest checks; in a dormitory, count the students as they enter the dining room; for an airline, count the passengers.

To make an estimate of how many customers will need to be fed, begin by taking a look at history and then formulate a guess. In the context of purchase forecasting, a "guess" is an estimate based on the forecaster's experience in general and knowledge of the business in particular, knowledge that usually results in a fairly accurate estimate.

Often the customer count at a special event will be provided, as when the head of the bowling banquet committee tells how many "high rollers" to expect. Sometimes, of course, there isn't any history to consult, such as when just beginning a new business. In this case, a guess at an expected customer count is both necessary and likely to be wrong, but it can be used as a good signpost for the next time. Most of the time, in restaurants, dormitories, in-plant food-services, and hospitals, the number to expect is approximately the number served in the past.

The method of forecasting customer counts that will be presented here is basically that of determining an average and adding a cushion for the unexpected. The cushion is the part of the forecast that is estimated. Three basic principles should be observed. First, be specific. For example, to forecast a customer count for next Tuesday's lunch, only refer to previous Tuesday lunches, not lunches for other days of the week. Second, consider an adequate amount of history. Following the above example, look at the last four or five Tuesday lunches and average them. For instance, assume the last five Tuesday lunch customer counts were as follows:

Jan. 3	Jan. 10	Jan. 17	Jan. 24	Jan. 31
217	200	206	188	215

The weekly average would then be 205.

Third is the matter of the cushion. How large a cushion should be added? The more widely the counts differ from the average, the larger the cushion should be. In the above example, each customer count was not much different from the others, so add a small cushion—say five—and estimate that 210 customers would need to be fed on February 7. This will minimize leftovers, and won't require too much scrambling if more guests than expected arrive. But consider the following situation:

Mar. 6	Mar. 13	Mar. 20	Mar. 27	Apr. 3
35	117	42	212	86

The average is 98, but it would be wise to add enough cushion to bring it up to at least 125, although even that increase might not be adequate on April 10. Remember that the size of the cushion depends on how widely each individual customer count differs from the others: a large difference, large cushion; a small difference, small cushion.

Here are a few examples of customer count forecasts:

May 2	May 9	May 16	May 23	May 30
512	488	513	520	501

Average = 507. Add a cushion of about 3 and plan on serving 510 on June 6.

Sept. 27	Oct. 4	Oct. 11	Oct. 18	Oct. 25
132	200	202	156	171

Average = 172. Add a cushion of 18 and plan on serving 190 on November 1.

There is no right or wrong answer to these cushion guesses; just use common sense. Too large a cushion can result in a lot of leftovers and a high food cost; too small a cushion could lead to angry customers. If historical customer counts fluctuate widely, it might be a good idea to revise the menu to use a lot of cook-to-order foods so there won't be a kitchen full of leftovers on any given night.

Computerizing Customer Count Forecasting

Forecasting customer count lends itself nicely to a spreadsheet program. Like almost any work on a spreadsheet, customer count can be set up many different ways. Page 34 contains one example. Take time to study it before proceeding any further.

Assume that the data recorded here are from a dormitory foodservice. As indicated earlier, the customer count for each meal period must be calculated independently. Notice that the data for each meal are divided into two parts, history and projections. Regarding history, the manager has apparently decided to base projections on the previous five weeks. This section of the sheet

Customers

requires no calculations, but is simply the place where customer count is recorded for this foodservice. Each day the manager or the helper records the actual customer count of the last breakfast, lunch, or dinner served (or perhaps someone will record all three at once the following day). Because the manager wants projections to reflect the latest five weeks of history, he or she must have the counts of the five previous same meals to work with. This can be done very simply. When any new counts are recorded, they are keyed in to replace the oldest date shown (note that the date indicated on the sample spreadsheet is the next date to be replaced by the new date and count). This way the worksheet always reflects the most recent five weeks of information.

The lower section of the worksheet deals with projection calculations. In this section the customer counts for the day in question are averaged, a cushion is added, and a forecast is made. Note that each day's projection is calculated separately because each day can be significantly different from the others in the week.

The average is the first thing to be calculated. All spreadsheet programs utilize arithmetic formulas, but they also make use of different mathematical functions. The formula used to calculate the average customer count for each day is one of those functions. Look at cell B21. The formula in that cell is: @ Avg (B5 . . F5). The @ in this program tells the computer to expect a formula containing a function. Avg is the function to be used in cell B21, and the cells from B5 to F5 are the ones to be averaged. Thus, this instruction placed in cell B21 tells the computer to average the values found in B5, C5, D5, E5, and F5, and

Forecasting Customer Count

Breakfast CC History

	04/05	04/12	03/15	03/22	03/29
Mon Date	04/05	04/12	03/15	03/22	03/29
CC	368	375	346	375	371
Tue Date	04/06	04/13	03/16	03/23	03/30
CC	342	381	372	381	366
Wed Date	04/07	04/14	03/17	03/24	03/31
CC	387	303	383	299	385
Thu Date	04/08	04/15	03/18	03/25	04/01
CC	376	362	394	357	361
Fri Date	04/09	04/16	03/19	03/26	04/02
CC	206	254	239	286	262
Sat Date	04/10	04/17	03/20	03/27	04/03
CC	158	109	136	122	179
Sun Date	04/11	04/18	03/21	03/28	04/04
CC	79	115	91	84	88

Forecasted Customer Count

	Average	SD	Cushion	Forecast
Mon	367	10	5	372
Tue	368	14	7	375
Wed	351	41	20	371
Thu	370	13	6	376
Fri	249	26	13	262
Sat	140	25	12	153
Sun	91	12	6	97

Lunch CC History

	04/05	04/12	03/15	03/22	03/29
Mon Date	04/05	04/12	03/15	03/22	03/29
CC	486	562	589	499	537
Tue Date	04/06	04/13	03/16	03/23	03/30
CC	502	498	536	547	488
Wed Date	04/07	04/14	03/17	03/24	03/31
CC	556	512	519	472	521
Thu Date	04/08	04/15	03/18	03/25	04/01
CC	490	563	571	567	511
Fri Date	04/09	04/16	03/19	03/26	04/02
CC	437	441	502	501	469
Sat Date	04/10	04/17	03/20	03/27	04/03
CC	418	365	422	398	377
Sun Date	04/11	04/18	03/21	03/28	04/04
CC	308	364	402	387	335

Forecasted Customer Count

	Average	SD	Cushion	Forecast
Mon	534	38	19	553
Tue	514	23	11	525
Wed	516	26	13	529
Thu	540	33	16	556
Fri	470	27	13	483
Sat	396	22	11	407
Sun	359	34	17	376

Dinner CC History

	04/05	04/12	03/15	03/22	03/29
Mon Date	04/05	04/12	03/15	03/22	03/29
CC	982	961	981	954	981
Tue Date	04/06	04/13	03/16	03/23	03/30
CC	956	899	872	911	962
Wed Date	04/07	04/14	03/17	03/24	03/31
CC	978	966	963	922	899
Thu Date	04/08	04/15	03/18	03/25	04/01
CC	941	972	899	901	961
Fri Date	04/09	04/16	03/19	03/26	04/02
CC	388	403	412	373	456
Sat Date	04/10	04/17	03/20	03/27	04/03
CC	141	215	167	182	236
Sun Date	04/11	04/18	03/21	03/28	04/04
CC	512	499	526	487	511

Forecasted Customer Count

	Average	SD	Cushion	Forecast
Mon	972	11	5	977
Tue	920	34	17	937
Wed	946	29	14	960
Thu	934	30	15	949
Fri	406	28	14	420
Sat	188	33	16	204
Sun	507	13	6	513

to record that average in cell number B21. The formula placed in cell B22 is just like it: @ Avg (B7 . . F7), and so on for cells B23–B27.

Column C in the calculations section of this worksheet is the standard deviation of the sample customer counts. Standard deviation is a statistical measurement of the variability of the sample from the sample's mean. Remember that it is suggested to build in a small cushion when customer counts are very similar to one another, and to provide a larger cushion when they are widely divergent. It gives the manager an idea of how different one of the historical customer counts is from the rest of the sample. From this measure of deviation, the manager can get an idea of how large the customer count cushion should be. Consequently, this spreadsheet has been programmed to calculate a standard deviation for each day's sample. Standard deviation is calculated in this program in the following way. Cell C21 contains the formula: @ SD (B5 . . F5), cell C22: @ SD (B7 . . F7), and so on.

The next column contains the cushion that the manager has decided to use. This can be selected in several ways. One way is for the manager to put in a cushion. He or she can look at the average and the sample's standard deviation and come up with a guess as to how large a cushion to include, and then record it in this column. In that case no calculations are necessary. Another way of providing for a cushion is to base it on the sample's standard deviation. This is what has been done in this example. The cushion for each day's forecast is one half of the day's standard deviation. So, the formula in cell number D21 is: C21/2 (the program being used doesn't round), the formula in cell D22 is: C22/2, and so on. For this projection the author elected to use one half of a standard deviation, but the cushion might just as easily have been three quarters or any part of a standard deviation. This method of forecasting is done simply to make the forecast of expected customer counts completely automatic.

The last column to program is the forecast itself. The program must be instructed to add the average customer count to the cushion selected for that forecast. Consequently, cell E21 = B21 + D21, cell E22 = B22 + D22, and so on. With this spreadsheet, a manager has only to record customer count history and forecasted customer counts are calculated automatically.

Problems

Here is the customer count history for the five previous weeks in a dormitory cafeteria:

	Sun.	Mon.	Tue.	Wed.	Thu.	Fri.	Sat.
Week #1							
Breakfast	10	256	227	248	229	187	75
Lunch	186	643	656	660	638	587	302
Dinner	407	852	903	881	893	489	252
Week #2							
Breakfast	3	241	248	252	243	203	186
Lunch	141	627	641	641	648	542	328
Dinner	388	887	884	910	881	506	308
Week #3							
Breakfast	12	274	256	233	261	209	134
Lunch	210	636	676	645	651	561	333
Dinner	392	874	884	897	897	481	327
Week #4							
Breakfast	12	267	200	248	254	197	97
Lunch	181	651	647	657	648	556	314
Dinner	395	881	892	893	899	498	526
Week #5							
Breakfast	8	243	271	261	256	188	156
Lunch	201	640	653	648	663	581	330
Dinner	401	897	871	876	903	510	551

Forecast the customer counts for the next

1. Sunday breakfast

2. Tuesday lunch

3. Wednesday dinner

4. Thursday lunch

5. Friday dinner

6. Saturday dinner

Chapter 6 Par Purchasing

OVERVIEW

When any part of a foodservice remains stable or changes infrequently, as in a sales menu used in a commercial restaurant, it is logical to expect the future to turn out like the past. In such cases, repeating past purchases should provide nicely for future needs. This chapter deals with two such stable situations: the constant use of staples in any foodservice (i.e., flour, sugar, spices, etc., that a business uses from week to week) and the unchanging sales menus that most restaurants use. Par purchasing was tailor-made for both of these situations. By arriving at an acceptable quantity expected for future orders, food can be purchased without calculating different forecasts for each order day.

KEY TERMS

> **Build-to**
> **Daily usage par**
> **Inventory**
> **Low-level par**
> **Par**
> **Usable inventory**

Establishing a Par

A **par** is usually an amount of food that will be enough for a given time period. For example, if two or three steaks are usually sold at a meal, a par of three steaks should suffice for any meal. A par is sometimes referred to as a **build-to** because, when ordering, enough is purchased to "build" to the amount required by the par. The word *par* has several meanings, of which this text will deal with two:

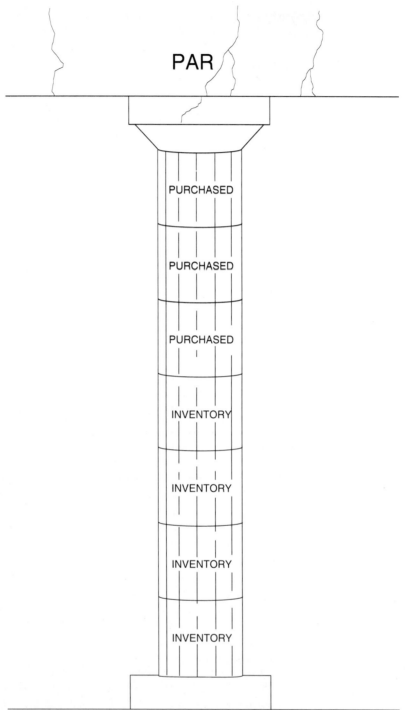

PAR

PURCHASED

PURCHASED

PURCHASED

INVENTORY

INVENTORY

INVENTORY

INVENTORY

Build to the Par

1. **Low-level par:** This is the smallest amount of an item on inventory that
   is acceptable on order day. This concept is usually used for staple items
   such as flour, sugar, coffee, and spices. It is an amount that experience
   has shown will last over a given purchasing period. A restaurant may
   find, for example, that 200 lb of flour will be enough for even the busiest
   week. If that's true, it's sufficient to keep a low-level par of 200 lb of flour
   on hand each ordering period. In other words, enough should be purchased on each weekly order to keep inventory at a minimum of 200 lb.

2. **Daily usage par:** This is the maximum amount that is likely to be used over the course of a day. A daily usage par could be good for any day of the week, or there could be two pars, one for the weekdays and one for the weekends. A daily usage par could even be calculated for each day of the week. This isn't difficult to do, especially with a computer.

Par establishment, like many other facets of forecasting, begins with history. Assume, for example, that daily usage pars are needed for the different items on the following steak menu:

9-oz New York strip

14-oz New York strip

10-oz Filet mignon

18-oz Porterhouse

8-oz Chopped steak

Since steaks probably aren't served to employees or wasted, a scatter sheet will give a fairly accurate picture of steak history. This scatter sheet shows activity for the previous two weeks:

Steak	S	M	T	W	T	F	S	S	M	T	W	T	F	S
9 oz	7	3	4	3	5	15	17	10	0	3	3	7	14	15
14 oz	20	11	14	9	9	27	36	22	7	9	6	8	125	30
Filet	15	8	0	7	7	18	22	11	5	7	8	6	12	14
Porter	11	4	2	1	2	9	75	8	6	2	2	2	12	17
Chopped	3	10	12	8	12	5	5	8	11	9	13	9	8	3

To formulate a daily usage par, pick the top usage recorded in history, *if it is normal,* and use that for the par estimate. What's *not* normal? Look at 14-oz strips. On the second Friday 125 of them were served. That's not even close to the rest of the 14-oz numbers. For some reason, perhaps a special party, consumption of 14-oz strips was unusually high on this day. A number like this shouldn't be used for par. The top daily usage par that is reasonable for these steaks is 36. Two pars would probably be more realistic; that is, 36 daily for Friday through Sunday and 14 daily for Monday through Thursday. To keep things simple though, a single par, 36 14-oz New York strip steaks, will be used. (*Note:* The average consumption for the two weeks could also be used as a par estimate. Remember, however, that using an average will cause a run-out about half of the time, and that's too often. Pick the top, normal usage for par.)

Picking the top usage for par helps to avoid run-out, but it can introduce another problem: using this forecasting method, there will be extra about half of the time. The danger of spoilage and resulting high food cost can be eliminated by careful rotation of stock using the FIFO (first in, first out) rule. *All stock should be rotated in storage automatically* so that spoilage will not be a problem, but this is particularly important when par purchasing.

Here are the pars established from the steak history provided. Verify the results for yourself.

Steak	*Daily Usage Par*
9-oz New York strip	17
14-oz New York strip	36
10-oz Filet mignon	22
18-oz Porterhouse	17
8-oz Chopped steak	13

Ordering with a Par

Once the pars are determined, they can be used for placing an order. Take a look at the following ordering pattern:

	Mon.	Tue.	Wed.	Thu.	Fri.	Sat.	Sun.	Mon.	Tue.
Order 1	ord.	del.	use	use	use			ord.	del.
Order 2				ord.	del.	use	use	use	use

Note that there are two steak deliveries per week, one on Tuesday covering Wednesday through Friday, and one on Friday covering Saturday through Tuesday. (*Note:* Don't plan to use any items on the day that they are to be delivered, since they might not arrive early enough to be used.) Here is how to formulate an order to be placed on Monday for a Tuesday delivery:

1. Multiply the daily usage par times the number of days the order is to cover. For 14-oz strips, this means 36 steaks for each of three days, or 108 steaks. (*Note:* You could have accomplished the same objective by counting pounds of steak, or even cases if need be, but dealing with the number of servings needed is more accurate.)

2. Build to 108 steaks by adjusting maximum projected needs for the three-day period. Remember, you won't need all 108 steaks unless it looks as though you will be out of them Wednesday morning (the first day that you plan to use these newly purchased steaks).

    For example, if you have 84 14-oz strips on hand on Monday morning, you could expect that 36 of those 84 steaks might be used later in the day and that 36 more might be used on Tuesday. That leaves 12 steaks on **usable inventory,** or available for use, on Wednesday. In other words, to calculate usable inventory, subtract from the initial inventory one daily usage par for each day from date of order up to the first day of usage. For Wednesday through Friday you will need a maximum of 108 steaks. You can therefore plan to buy 108 minus 12, or 96 steaks. Remember, of the 84 steaks on inventory only 12 will be on usable inventory come Wednesday. Notice the difference between the terms *inventory* and *usable inventory*. **Inventory** is the amount of food on hand on order day, while usable inventory is used to adjust a daily usage par. If you buy 96 steaks, this will be plenty for Wednesday, Thursday, and Friday, and you will probably have some left over to become usable inventory on Saturday. If stock is rotated this won't be a problem.

    It is important to understand that, when par purchasing, the entire par amount is seldom purchased. Build to it and purchase the difference between the amount derived from the par requirements and usable inventory. (*Note:* If the established par is consistently too large or small, change it. Start with the top usage to avoid run-out, but adjust the par up or down to reflect need.)

Menu Types and Par Forecasting

As mentioned, use of a low-level par is best suited for keeping an adequate supply of staples on hand, regardless of expected business. Experience will teach how large your low-level par should be. A low-level par is useful for any menu situation because a kitchen will always use staple items, and the type of menu has little to do with how much of a staple will be needed.

A daily usage par *does* depend on menu. For example, there is no need to have a par for items ordered only once. Similarly, a daily usage par doesn't work well for a cycle menu. The daily usage par was tailor-made for sales menus that remain virtually unchanged day after day, since they require purchasing the same kind of items for each order.

▨▨▨▨▨ EXAMPLE

Given the following Thursday morning inventory, how much will you need to order for the Friday steak delivery? (Remember that the Friday delivery covers four days of use.)

Steak	Inventory
9-oz New York strip	40
14-oz New York strip	102
10-oz Filet mignon	61
18-oz Porterhouse	30
8-oz Chopped steak	26

Solution

(daily usage par × number of days) – usable inventory = order.

9-oz New York strip	$(17 \times 4) - 6 = 62$
14-oz New York strip	$(36 \times 4) - 30 = 114$
10-oz Filet mignon	$(22 \times 4) - 17 = 71$
18-oz Porterhouse	$(17 \times 4) - 0 = 68$
8-oz Chopped steak	$(13 \times 4) - 0 = 52$

(*Note:* You may run out of Porterhouse steaks on Friday, so it's acceptable to add enough of them to take up the slack on this order. Since the run-out would be likely to occur during the evening meal, the newly purchased steaks will probably arrive in time.)

As long as storage is organized with FIFO in mind all of the time, par purchasing works well in most restaurant situations. However, spoilage and a high food cost will result if one doesn't rotate stock and follow the FIFO rule every time.

Computerizing the Daily Usage Par

In the previous discussion a par was established that would be sufficient for any day of the week, one par for the business's seven different daily needs. Although keeping a lot of numbers straight is tedious, a par specific to *each* day of the week provides for much more accurate purchasing. With a computer, a par specific to each day of the week is easily established. The spreadsheet provided on page 44 illustrates how pars specific to individual daily consumption can be used to forecast. Imagine that the data presented come from the steak portion of the menu of a moderately priced family restaurant. Study the spreadsheet to see how it works.

Just as individual pars are used for different foods as previously discussed, different pars are used for each kind of steak when a computer is used. Therefore, the same program used to forecast the Porterhouse steak order is repeated for each of the other types of steak.

The data on the spreadsheet in the range A4 to F17 are very much like the first section of the customer count worksheet. It is a record of history, but instead of customer counts, Porterhouse steak usage is recorded. In this case,

Daily Usage Par Worksheet

	A	B	C	D	E	F	G	H	I	J	K	L	M	N	O	P	Q	R	S	T	U
			Porterhouse				D U Par		Filet Mignon					D U Par		New York Strip					D U Par
4	Mon Date	04/05	04/12	03/15	03/22	03/29		Mon Date	04/05	04/12	03/15	03/22	03/29		Mon Date	04/05	04/12	03/15	03/22	03/29	
5	Usage	5	3	11	0	6	11	Usage	3	7	5	6	2	7	Usage	13	14	11	11	13	14
6	Tue Date	04/06	04/13	03/16	03/23	03/30		Tue Date	04/06	04/13	03/16	03/23	03/30		Tue Date	04/06	04/13	03/16	03/23	03/30	
7	Usage	7	1	9	8	4	9	Usage	4	4	7	12	8	12	Usage	9	15	13	15	11	15
8	Wed Date	04/07	04/14	03/17	03/24	03/31		Wed Date	04/07	04/14	03/17	03/24	03/31		Wed Date	04/07	04/14	03/17	03/24	03/31	
9	Usage	14	7	9	11	12	14	Usage	9	6	15	12	8	15	Usage	14	12	14	11	13	14
10	Thu Date	04/08	04/15	03/18	03/25	04/01		Thu Date	04/08	04/15	03/18	03/25	04/01		Thu Date	04/08	04/15	03/18	03/25	04/01	
11	Usage	9	12	8	10	6	12	Usage	11	18	16	11	17	18	Usage	12	13	11	17	14	17
12	Fri Date	04/09	04/16	03/19	03/26	04/02		Fri Date	04/09	04/16	03/19	03/26	04/02		Fri Date	04/09	04/16	03/19	03/26	04/02	
13	Usage	16	17	12	7	16	17	Usage	23	16	23	20	21	23	Usage	27	31	37	32	32	37
14	Sat Date	04/10	04/17	03/20	03/27	04/03		Sat Date	04/10	04/17	03/20	03/27	04/03		Sat Date	04/10	04/17	03/20	03/27	04/03	
15	Usage	20	21	19	16	18	21	Usage	18	20	19	27	22	27	Usage	31	30	42	38	38	42
16	Sun Date	04/11	04/18	03/21	03/28	04/04		Sun Date	04/11	04/18	03/21	03/28	04/04		Sun Date	04/11	04/18	03/21	03/28	04/04	
17	Usage	13	9	11	14	11	14	Usage	22	19	22	21	22	22	Usage	36	27	28	26	33	36
18																					
19	Current Inventory		30					Current Inventory		63					Current Inventory		38				
20																					
21			Build to	Extra	U I					Build to	Extra	U I					Build to	Extra	U I		
22	Forecast W,T,F		43	0	10			Forecast W,T,F		56	25	44			Forecast W,T,F		68	0	9		
23																					
24	Forecast S,S,M,T		55	36	1			Forecast S,S,M,T		68	36	22			Forecast S,S,M,T		107	36	–16		
25																					
26			Porter	Filet	NY Strip																
27	Mon Order		33	37	59																
28																					
29	Thu Order		90	82	159																

44

as in the customer count worksheet, the manager has elected to keep track of the previous five weeks of history. No calculations are used in this area of either worksheet. Each time current history is recorded, the newest material replaces the oldest so that the most current five weeks of history are always displayed.

The first calculations encountered on this worksheet are in column G. Most spreadsheet programs have a function called MAX that selects the greatest value from a collection of numbers. The formulas in column G are @ MAX (B5..F5) in cell G5, @ MAX (B7..F7) in cell G7, and so on. Pars in this example are selected by finding the top usage in history. Note that these formulas select a par to be used for each day, not one for the whole week.

Each time the manager orders, the actual, not usable, inventory is recorded in cell C19 at the time of forecast. The computer can easily be programmed to convert actual inventories to usable inventories, so only the actual figure needs to be recorded here.

In this example, forecasts are developed to provide for the following order/delivery/use schedule:

	Mon.	Tue.	Wed.	Thu.	Fri.	Sat.	Sun.	Mon.	Tue.
Order 1	ord.	del.	use	use	use			ord.	del.
Order 2				ord.	del.	use	use	use	use

When a daily usage par is used to forecast, forecasts begin with the maximum number of items—in this case Porterhouse steaks—that will be needed for the time period considered. Therefore, the first thing that needs to be calculated using this method of forecast is the build-to. The first forecast to develop is for use on Wednesday, Thursday, and Friday. So cell C22 contains the sum of the daily usage (DU) pars for Wednesday, Thursday, and Friday; that is, G9 + G11 + G13. The build-to for the next order should be comprised of the daily usage pars for Saturday, Sunday, Monday, and Tuesday; that is, cell C24 = G5 + G7 + G15 + G17.

Cells D22 and D24, the ones labeled "Extra," are those extra steaks that the manager may need for a special party. No calculations are needed for these cells, but they must be included in the final order.

The data contained in cells E22 and E24 are the usable inventories (UI) needed to calculate the final orders. To set up the instructions for these two cells, the manager has used the following logic. The first steak order will be prepared Monday morning or afternoon. Most steaks are consumed at dinner, not at lunch, so regardless of when on Monday the steaks are inventoried, most of them will still be there for consumption Monday evening. So, the difference between actual inventory and usable inventory will usually be Monday's and Tuesday's par. The usable inventory to be used in the first forecast, cell E22, is C19 − G5 − G7. Similarly, the usable inventory used in the second forecast, E24, is C19 − G11 − G13. Thus, when the manager records the actual inventory at the time of forecast, the spreadsheet will calculate usable inventory automatically.

Last of all, the final order must be assembled. The number of steaks to build to is added to any amount of extra steaks needed for special parties, and the total is then adjusted for usable inventory. Therefore, cells C27 and C29 contain the formulas C22 + D22 − E22 and C24 + D24 − E24, respectively. Cell D27 is prepared in the same way. It contains the formula J22 + K22 − L22. Note that cell S24 is negative. That means that the business is likely to run out of New York strip steaks sometime Friday night, and if the manager doesn't want to run out he or she must order 16 extra. (They should be received in time, since they will probably not be needed until evening.) In order to use this spreadsheet to forecast the steak needs with a daily usage par, the manager must do three things: (1) update the historic steak usage, (2) record the number of steaks on hand at the time, and (3) record any special steak needs. The program does the rest.

Problems

As the new assistant manager of a deli, you are responsible for the bread order. Look at the scatter sheet summary on page 48, and first formulate pars for these baked goods:

1. White bread at 22 usable slices per loaf.

2. Wheat bread at 22 usable slices per loaf.

3. Oval rye bread at 13 usable slices per loaf.

Menu Scatter Sheet

Sandwich	Mon	Tue	Wed	Thu	Fri	Sat	Sun	Mon	Tue	Wed	Thu	Fri	Sat	Sun
Beef on white	15	13	17	13	20	26	22	18	16	14	15	18	28	21
Beef on wheat	3	0	7	6	8	10	11	8	6	3	5	6	8	10
Beef on rye	18	23	19	19	23	36	34	17	17	23	20	24	33	37
Beef on kaiser	37	28	31	33	46	86	49	22	37	33	38	41	48	42
Beef on onion	26	26	28	30	36	38	41	21	19	23	24	37	42	38
Turkey on white	18	16	18	23	18	26	23	16	15	18	21	24	26	24
Turkey on wheat	17	23	18	19	23	31	34	18	21	15	16	23	32	30
Turkey on rye	2	6	4	7	10	12	11	0	6	7	6	13	15	11
Turkey on kaiser	18	17	19	15	23	31	33	22	18	21	21	23	30	33
Turkey on onion	16	13	5	18	21	26	25	19	24	16	17	18	22	83
Ham on white	24	16	19	22	31	46	43	19	27	23	24	18	41	38
Ham on wheat	33	27	28	36	28	42	47	21	21	26	23	27	45	41
Ham on rye	34	31	36	38	43	58	62	32	39	42	36	54	64	59
Ham on kaiser	27	18	29	31	26	46	37	31	28	26	39	42	47	41
Ham on onion	18	12	14	16	31	27	26	18	17	103	27	26	25	31
Corned beef on white	0	0	0	13	12	15	21	16	12	8	15	16	16	13
Corned beef on wheat	7	18	11	6	23	26	13	9	10	8	12	21	26	24
Corned beef on rye	24	18	19	25	37	41	43	18	19	26	24	31	40	38
Corned beef on kaiser	25	27	18	27	29	46	43	9	27	18	33	37	41	45
Corned beef on onion	17	15	15	22	18	31	32	23	16	21	23	31	30	28
Pastrami on white	1	0	3	6	7	13	12	0	0	7	11	4	10	8
Pastrami on wheat	7	14	15	13	21	25	24	14	12	12	18	16	23	19
Pastrami on rye	37	35	27	36	38	52	56	31	47	18	38	41	53	55
Pastrami on kaiser	36	29	31	33	37	48	53	31	33	21	34	46	57	46
Pastrami on onion	24	25	18	24	31	47	41	29	27	30	36	39	41	48
Italian on bun	18	16	18	21	19	27	21	6	16	15	21	23	25	23
Hot dog on bun	56	63	64	51	82	97	101	41	51	48	55	56	93	96
Polish on bun	18	23	14	14	13	21	26	8	0	17	24	18	23	13
Chili dog on bun	37	28	39	42	42	58	49	27	34	38	41	58	56	53

4. Kaiser rolls at 12 rolls per package.

5. Onion rolls at 12 rolls per package.

6. Hot dog buns at 10 buns per package.

Now that you have bread pars, order bread for Saturday, Sunday, and Monday. You will call in the order early Friday morning, and it will be delivered before you open on Saturday, so you can use it for business on Saturday. Before you open on Friday your bread inventory is as follows:

White	18 loaves
Wheat	19 loaves
Oval rye	28 loaves
Kaiser	25 packages
Onion	15 packages
Hot dog buns	31 packages

How much will you need to order for:

7. White bread

8. Wheat bread

9. Rye bread

10. Kaiser rolls

11. Onion rolls

12. Hot dog buns

Chapter 7 Usage Ratio

OVERVIEW

Because most operations that utilize a cycle menu serve the same customers with some regularity, it is possible for the management to identify these guests' food preferences. One of the benefits of a cycle menu is that it offers menu items in the same combinations with one another time after time. By studying historic usage, it is possible to determine the amount of food that a single guest might consume on the average. With this information, it is a simple matter to increase the requirements of the average customer to the requirements of the total number of customers expected.

KEY TERMS

Equal cycle

Long cycle

Usage ratio

Equal Cycles and Long Cycles

As stated in Chapter 1, cycle menus usually consist of as many menus as there are days to cover. For instance, if a business is open five days per week and wants the cycle to cover four weeks, a collection of twenty daily menus is written and then repeated every four weeks. This is called an **equal cycle.** This is probably the most used type of cycle menu. It works, but may contribute to the boredom that can occur when cycle menus are used.

Forecasting is relatively easy when dealing with an equal cycle. In cycle type operations, customer counts are often similar from one Wednesday to the next, or from one Saturday dinner to the next, as in an in-plant situation. Since the same people will be there to eat the food, and will be there in similar numbers, usage one time through the cycle will usually be about the same when the cycle is repeated. To forecast in this situation, keep accurate history, usually in the form of a production sheet.

Any in-plant or school lunch program manager knows that boredom breeds dissatisfaction and eventual loss of customers. If the cycle is designed to be longer than the number of days it is to cover, the pattern will be much harder for guests to identify. For example, if one wants a cycle to cover four seven-day weeks, write 31 or 32 menus rather than 28, and the cycle will skip days as it is repeated. This variety of cycle menu is called a **long cycle.** This offers the benefit of a cycle menu, since items repeat themselves in the same combinations each time the cycle is repeated (history is thus reliable), but much of the boredom is eliminated because the menu pattern is much harder to anticipate.

Usage Ratio

Many establishments that use a cycle menu have a high degree of repeat customers, and these repeats tend to exhibit a sort of "eating personality," or similar eating habits from one time through the cycle to the next. A **usage ratio,** which recognizes this characteristic, provides an average consumption per guest (not for the total usage of the meal).

Calculating the Usage Ratio

The formula for finding a usage ratio is as follows:

$$\text{Usage ratio} = \frac{\text{actual (historical) total usage}}{\text{actual (historical) customer count}}$$

At the conclusion of each meal, the production sheet is completed as usual, but for a usage ratio an additional step will be taken. Here is a sample production sheet:

Sunday	Actual Customer Count	Actual Usage
Roast beef	435	107 lb
Burrito		¾ case
Chicken chow mein		78 servings (S)

(*Note:* Keep track of usage in whatever form is most convenient, depending on the item.)

To find an entrée's usage ratio, divide its actual usage by the meal's actual customer count. For roast beef,

$$\frac{107 \text{ lb}}{435 \text{ cust.}} = 0.246 \text{ lb per cust.}$$

Continuing, the result is

Item	Usage	Usage Ratio
Roast beef	107 lb	0.246 lb/cust.
Burrito	¾ case	0.002 cases/cust.
Chicken chow mein	78 S	0.179 S/cust.

(*Note:* Observe that the label on the usage ratio is similar to the way that the history was recorded.)

The above calculated usage ratios indicate that, on an average, each customer ate 0.246 pounds of roast beef, 0.002 cases of burritos, and 0.179 servings of chow mein. The usage ratio then is a usage figure, independent of attendance, showing what an average customer consumed. Carry these calculations out to four decimal places and then round them back to three places to get the needed accuracy.

The Average Guest at the Company's In-Plant Cafeteria Comes Home for Dinner

Remember, with an equal cycle forecasts are a lot like previous usage, but with a long cycle forecasts are more complicated. Day one of a long cycle may be Sunday the first time through, but may show up as a Wednesday the next time through. In a dorm, for instance, Wednesdays are usually much busier than Sundays. The same people are fed on both days, but a far greater number of them are fed on Wednesdays. Their eating habits have been built into the usage ratio.

Putting the Usage Ratio to Work

When the cycle is repeated, usage must be forecast in order to plan purchases and production. The first thing that is needed for this is a forecasted customer count. Recall that a forecasted customer count is an average of the actual customer counts for the previous same meals, with a cushion added if necessary. Let's say that the forecasted customer count for the Wednesday in question comes out to be 950 customers, and that usage ratios are on record for the first time through the cycle. To forecast, multiply a menu item's usage ratio times the forecasted customer count:

Menu item forecast = usage ratio × forecasted customer count

Based on the little menu just given, the roast beef forecast for Wednesday is

$$\frac{0.246 \text{ lb}}{\text{cust.}} \times 950 \text{ cust.} = 233.7, \text{ or about } 234 \text{ lb}$$

Remember a usage ratio is the average amount of food that one is served, so if 950 customers are expected, 950 times 0.246 lb of beef will be needed. The forecast for the meal then becomes:

Item	Usage Ratio	Forecasted CC	Forecast
Beef	0.246 lb/cust.	950	234 lb
Burrito	0.002 cases/cust.	950	1.9 cases
Chow mein	0.179 S	950	170 S

A cushion can be added, but it isn't necessary. A usage ratio will change a little from one time through the cycle to the next, but all in all it is a wonderful tool for forecasting from a long cycle menu.

Computerizing Usage Ratio Forecasting

Usage ratio calculations can easily be done on a spreadsheet. The example on page 55 is one way this type of forecasting can be computerized. The data dealt with here are from a five days per week, lunch only, high school cafeteria. The example shows a twenty-four menu cycle designed to cover a twenty-day, four-week period. Column A contains the number of each of the 24 menus comprising the cycle; column B lists the actual menus; column C is the portion size served to each student; and columns D, E, and F are the recorded history of meals already served. Notice that the material in column F has been assembled in terms of the labels shown in column G and not necessarily in the same terms as the portion size. This historic usage has been recorded in the terms given because it was easiest for the production staff to record the meals' actual usage in these ways. The rectangle containing the recorded history indicates the material that needs to be updated in order to calculate the menu's usage ratios.

Column H is the first one that requires calculations. It contains the following formulas: H5 = F5/E5, H6 = F6/E5, H7 = F7/E7, H8 = F8/E7, H9 = F9/E9, and H10 = F10/E9, and so on. Usage ratios equal historic usage divided by historic customer count. Columns I and J contain the data, forecast dates, and forecasted customer counts that the manager must input to enable the computer to make future usage projections. If the manager had a more sophisticated spreadsheet than this one, he or she could probably have linked the customer count worksheet to columns D and E, and I and J, of this usage ratio worksheet, and the date and customer count information, both historic and forecasted, could be entered automatically. If these dates and customer counts were recorded automatically, the manager would only have to enter the usage information in column F to supply the necessary information for the program.

Now that the computer has all of that information at its disposal, the usage ratio can be used to forecast. Historic usage divided by historic customer count provides the menu's usage ratios, and those usage ratios multiplied by the forecasted customer count provides the forecast. Not only has the forecast been calculated in this column, but that forecast has been converted to usable units at the same time. By comparing the labels in columns G and L, it can be seen how the labels used in recording history have been changed into the labels of the usable units desired.

Column K is by far the most complicated on this worksheet. The formulas in the cells are comprised of three different parts:

1. They contain the forecast, which is the menu item's usage ratio multiplied by the forecasted customer count.

2. They contain the needed calculations for converting these forecasts to usable units.

Usage Ratio Worksheet

Day	Entree	Unit	Hist Date	Hist CC	Hist Use	Label	Use Ratio	Fore Date	Fore CC	Forecast	Label
1	FF Chix	1 quarter	Mo 02/17	963	503	quarter	0.5223	Fr 03/21	827	108	head
	BBQ Pork	4 oz EP			115	lb EP	0.1194			152	lb AP
2	Pizza	1/6 pie	Tu 02/18	981	102	14" pie	0.1039	Mo 03/24	958	100	14" pie
	Hot Dog	8/1			52	lb AP	0.0530			51	lb AP
3	Hamburger	5/1	We 02/19	975	149	lb AP	0.1528	Tu 03/25	930	143	lb AP
	A Goulash	6 oz/S			234	S	0.2400			8	recipes
4	Spaghetti	4 oz/S	Th 02/20	978	603	S	0.6165	We 03/26	970	12	recipes
	Fish n Chips	4 oz AP			107	lb AP	0.1094			107	lb AP
5	Meat Loaf	4 oz/S	Fr 02/21	813	399	S	0.4907	Th 03/27	912	18	recipes
	C Stir-Fry	6 oz/S			420	S	0.5166			12	recipes
6	R Beef	4 oz/S	Mo 02/24	1002	106	lb EP	0.1057	Fr 03/28	846	128	lb AP
	BLT	2 oz AP			71	lb AP	0.0708			60	lb AP
7	Pizza	1/6 pie	Tu 02/25	969	119	14" pie	0.1228	Mo 03/31	1004	124	14" pie
	Tuna Melt	#12 scoop			256	S	0.2641			8	recipes
8	FF Chix	1 quarter	We 02/26	983	348	quarter	0.3540	Tu 04/01	989	88	head
	Tacos	1 oz/S			675	S	0.6866			14	recipes
9	P Sausage	4 oz AP	Th 02/27	971	77	lb AP	0.0792	We 04/02	942	75	lb AP
	Lasagna	6 oz/S			682	S	0.7023			23	recipes
10	G Cheese	1 oz sand	Fr 02/28	838	502	sandwiches	0.5990	Th 04/03	961	576	sandwiches
	Chili	8 oz/S			346	S	0.4128			8	recipes
11	Hamburger	5/1	Mo 03/03	948	126	lb AP	0.1329	Fr 04/04	816	109	lb AP
	C Tenders	4 oz			16.5	boxes	0.0174			2	cases
12	Burritos	3 oz/S	Tu 03/04	977	20.75	boxes	0.0212	Mo 04/07	962	6	cases
	Fish n Chips	4 oz AP			127	lb AP	0.1299			126	lb AP
13	Pizza	1/6 pie	We 03/05	963	85	14" pie	0.0882	Tu 04/08	1001	89	14" pie
	Sloppy Joe	#12 scoop			461	S	0.4787			16	recipes
14	Spaghetti	4 oz/S	Th 03/06	990	511	S	0.5161	We 04/09	965	10	recipes
	R Beef	4 oz EP			123	lb EP	0.1242			172	lb AP
15	Reuben	2 oz/sand	Fr 03/07	832	504	sandwiches	0.6057	Th 04/10	971	589	sandwiches
	Pork Chop	4 oz AP			85	lb AP	0.1021			100	lb AP
16	FF Shrimp	4 oz/S	Mo 03/10	915	41	boxes	0.0448	Fr 04/11	873	4	cases
	Hot Dogs	8/1			34	lb AP	0.0371			33	lb AP
17	FF Chix	1 quarter	Tu 03/11	948	736	quarters	0.7763	Mo 04/14	915	178	head
	I Sausage	4 oz AP			53	lb AP	0.0559			52	lb AP
18	Tacos	1 oz/S	We 03/12	972	735	S	0.7561	Tu 04/15	946	15	recipes
	Ham	4 oz EP			60	S	0.0617			65	lb AP
19	Pizza	1/6 pie	Th 03/13	947	80	14" pie	0.0844	We 04/16	953	81	14" pie
	BLT	2 oz AP			59	lb EP	0.0623			60	lb AP
20	Turk & Dres	4 oz EP	Fr 03/14	800	109	lb EP	0.1362	Th 04/17	974	145	lb AP
	Span Rice	6 oz/S			436	S	0.5450			9	recipes
21	Moussaka	6 oz/S	Mo 03/17	938	314	S	0.3347	Fr 04/18	838	8	recipes
	Submarine	6 oz/sand			636	sandwiches	0.6780			569	sandwiches
22	Ital Beef	4 oz EP	Tu 03/18	961	177	lb EP	0.1841	Mo 04/21	911	240	lb AP
	P Fr Rice	6 oz/S			263	S	0.2736			8	recipes
23	Ravioli	4 oz/S	We 03/19	957	37	#10 cans	0.0386	Tu 04/22	952	7	cases
	FF Clams	4 oz/S			12	boxes	0.0125			2	cases
24	C a la King	6 oz/S	Th 03/20	953	206	S	0.2161	We 04/23	941	5	recipes
	Stromboli	4 oz/sand			747	sandwiches	0.7838			738	sandwiches

3. Since this program doesn't round numbers, 1 has been added to each projection so as not to leave anyone short.

The cells in column K therefore contain the following formulas:

Cell	Formula	Explanation
K5	(H5*j5/4)+1	4 quarters to a head
K6	(H6*j5/.65)+1	AP yield is 65%
K7	(H7*J7)+1	
K8	(H8*J7)+1	
K9	(H9*J9)+1	
K10	(H10*J9/30)+1	30 S is the recipe yield
K11	(H11*J11/50)+1	50 S is the recipe yield
K12	(H12*J11)+1	
K13	(H13*J13/25)+1	25 S is the recipe yield
K14	(H14*J13/40)+1	40 S is the recipe yield
K15	(H15*J15/.7)+1	AP yield is 70%
K16	(H16*J15)+1	
K17	(H17*J17)+1	
K18	(H18*J17/36)+1	36 S is the recipe yield
K19	(H19*J19/4)+1	4 quarters to a head
K20	(H20*J19/50)+1	50 S is the recipe yield
K21	(H21*J21)+1	
K22	(H22*J21/30)+1	30 S is the recipe yield
K23	(H23*J23)+1	
K24	(H24*J23/50)+1	50 S is the recipe yield
K25	(H25*J25)+1	
K26	(H26*J25/10)+1	10 boxes per case
K27	(H27*J27/4)+1	4 boxes per case
K28	(H28*J27)+1	
K29	(H29*J29)+1	
K30	(H30*J29/30)+1	30 S is the recipe yield
K31	(H31*J31/50)+1	50 S is the recipe yield
K32	(H32*J31/.7)+1	AP yield is 70%
K33	(H33*J33)+1	
K34	(H34*J33)+1	
K35	(H35*J35/10)+1	10 boxes per case
K36	(H36*J35)+1	
K37	(H37*J37/4)+1	4 quarters to a head
K38	(H38*J37)+1	
K39	(H39*J39/50)+1	50 S is the recipe yield
K40	(H40*J39/.9)+1	AP yield is 90%
K41	(H41*J41)+1	
K42	(H42*J41)+1	
K43	(H43*J43/.92)+1	AP yield is 92%
K44	(H44*J43/65)+1	65 S is the recipe yield
K45	(H45*J45/40)+1	40 S is the recipe yield
K46	(H46*J45)+1	
K47	(H47*J47/.7)+1	AP yield is 70%
K48	(H48*J47/35)+1	35 S is the recipe yield
K49	(H49*J49/6)+1	6 #10 cans per case
K50	(H50*J49/10)+1	10 boxes per case
K51	(H51*J51/45)+1	45 S is the recipe yield
K52	(H52*J51)+1	

With this worksheet the manager need only update history and input forecasted customer counts to obtain forecasts for the upcoming menus in terms that are useful. While this worksheet takes some effort to set up initially, it generates forecasts with ease.

Problems

1. Below is a production sheet summary with actual customer counts from an "all you can eat" dormitory foodservice, using a long cycle. Calculate the usage ratios for this part of the cycle, and record them on the answer sheet on page 61. Then forecast the food for the next time, given the forecasted customer counts supplied.

Menu Item	Actual Customer Count	Historical Usage
Sunday Week 1	417	
F F chicken		98 head
Sweet & sour pork		138 S
Ham & cheese sandwich		217 each
Monday Week 1	836	
Roast beef		218 lb AP
Chicken pot pie		136 S
Stuffed pepper		89 S
Tuesday Week 1	850	
Pork chops		756 each
Arroz con pollo		94 S
Meat loaf		283 S
Wednesday Week 1	841	
Spaghetti & meat sauce		528 S
Turkey & dressing		64 lb AP
Corned beef & cabbage		53 lb AP
Thursday Week 1	873	
Hamburger		927 S
F F clams		3.5 boxes
Pepper steak		78 S
Friday Week 1	647	
Baked salmon		83 lb AP
Beef stroganoff		192 S
Sloppy Joe		64 S
Saturday Week 1	308	
Pizza		78 14″
Baked ham		13 lb AP
Chicken chow mein		52 S

2. Below is a production sheet summary for a "type A" high school lunch program, also using a long cycle. It contains actual usage and customer counts from part of the twenty-five-day cycle in use there. Calculate the usage ratios for this time through the cycle, and then forecast the food for the next time through. Use the answer sheet on page 62.

Menu Item	Actual Customer Count	Historical Usage
Monday Week 1	742	
Hamburger		518 S
Turkey & dressing		31 lb AP
Pork fried rice		87 S
Tuesday Week 1	731	
Grilled ham & cheese		496 S
Fish & chips		43 lb AP
Meat loaf		63 S
Wednesday Week 1	762	
Pizza		171 12″
Ham & scalloped potatoes		34 S
Chili		49 S
Thursday Week 1	704	
Sloppy Joe		423 S
Chicken tenders		4 boxes
Beef stew		187 S
Friday Week 1	659	
Beef burrito		12.5 boxes
Spaghetti & meat sauce		312 S
Baked white fish		17 lb AP

**Problem #1
Answer Sheet**

Menu Item	Forecasted Customer Count	Usage Ratio	Food Forecast
Tuesday Week 1	875		
F F chicken		_____	_____
Sweet & sour pork		_____	_____
Ham & cheese sandwich		_____	_____
Wednesday Week 1	850		
Roast beef		_____	_____
Chicken pot pie		_____	_____
Stuffed pepper		_____	_____
Thursday Week 1	895		
Pork chops		_____	_____
Arroz con pollo		_____	_____
Meat loaf		_____	_____
Friday Week 1	640		
Spaghetti & meat sauce		_____	_____
Turkey & dressing		_____	_____
Corned beef & cabbage		_____	_____
Saturday Week 1	325		
Hamburger		_____	_____
F F clams		_____	_____
Pepper steak		_____	_____
Sunday Week 1	435		
Baked salmon		_____	_____
Beef stroganoff		_____	_____
Sloppy Joe		_____	_____
Monday Week 1	845		
Pizza		_____	_____
Baked ham		_____	_____
Chicken chow mein		_____	_____

**Problem #2
Answer Sheet**

Menu Item	Forecasted Customer Count	Usage Ratio	Food Forecast
Wednesday Week 1	745		
Hamburger		_____	_____
Turkey & dressing		_____	_____
Pork fried rice		_____	_____
Thursday Week 1	730		
Grilled ham & cheese		_____	_____
Fish & chips		_____	_____
Meat loaf		_____	_____
Friday Week 1	675		
Pizza		_____	_____
Ham & scalloped potatoes		_____	_____
Chili		_____	_____
Monday Week 1	755		
Sloppy Joe		_____	_____
Chicken tenders		_____	_____
Beef stew		_____	_____
Tuesday Week 1	750		
Beef burrito		_____	_____
Spaghetti & meat sauce		_____	_____
Baked white fish		_____	_____

Chapter **8** *Forecasting Using Customer Count x Portion Size*

OVERVIEW

In any catering situation, when all of the guests will be served the same menu items, the supply needs of the group are determined by multiplying the individual portion size times the number of customers expected.

KEY TERM

Portion size

Customer Count x Portion Size

Forecasted customer counts are the starting point for many forecasting techniques. Probably the simplest method of forecasting with an estimated customer count is to multiply the expected customer count times the **portion size**—the amount that each customer will receive:

$$\underset{\substack{Customer \\ Count}}{515 \text{ people}} \times \underset{\substack{Portion \\ Size}}{\frac{3 \text{ oz}}{\text{person}}} = 1545 \text{ oz}$$

or

$$\underset{\substack{Customer \\ Count}}{275 \text{ people}} \times \underset{\substack{Portion \\ Size}}{\frac{2 \text{ servings}}{\text{person}}} \times \frac{1.5 \text{ oz}}{\text{serving}} = 825 \text{ oz}$$

This method of forecasting can work with any type of menu, but it was tailor-made for a special event menu situation. It will most often yield an AS

Customer Count x Portion Size Equals Total Forecast

result, since portion size is usually expressed in AS terms. If portion size is an AP amount, however, the result will also be AP.

Computerizing Forecasting Using Customer Count x Portion Size

Forecasting with customer count times portion size is about the simplest of all the techniques presented in this workbook. Since the operation only takes one step of multiplication, it is not really worth setting up a spreadsheet to forecast in this way. But portion size is something that must be recorded, so that information can also be used as a forecasting device for customer count times portion size.

	A	B	C	D	E	F	G
1	**CC * Portion Size**						
2							
3	Forecasted Customer Count			875			
4							
5	Entree		Portion	Forecast	Label	Adj Fore	Label
6	Beef stir-fry		8 oz	875	S	26	recipes
7	Beef stroganoff		8 oz	875	S	44	recipes
8	Filet mignon		10 oz EP	546	lb EP	644	lb AP
9	New York strip		10 oz EP	546	lb EP	667	lb AP
10	Prime rib		12 oz EP	656	lb EP	912	lb AP
11	Roast round of beef		7 oz EP	382	lb EP	547	lb AP
12	Pork chops		2-4 oz EP	437	lb EP	626	lb AP
13	Roast pork loin		7 oz EP	382	lb EP	589	lb AP
14	Sweet & sour pork		8 oz	875	S	36	recipes
15	Chicken cordon bleu		7 oz	875	eaches	10	cases
16	Chicken kiev		7 oz	875	eaches	10	cases
17	Chicken stir-fry		8 oz	875	S	59	recipes
18	Honey fried chicken		1 quarter	875	quarters	219	head
19	Turkey divan		10 oz	875	S	44	recipes
20	Turkey & dressing		7 oz	382	lb EP	417	lb AP
21	Grilled salmon		8 oz EP	437	lb EP	663	lb AP
22	Dover sole almondine		8 oz EP	437	lb EP	608	lb AP
23	Lobster tail		10 oz	875	eaches	73	cases
24	Shrimp De Jong		8 oz	875	S	18	recipes
25	Fettuccini Alfredo		4 oz	875	S	22	recipes
26	Lasagna		10 oz	875	S	19	recipes
27	Spaghetti & meat sauce	4 oz		27	gal	11	recipes
28							
29							

On the worksheet shown on page 64 are listed all of the entrées that a certain catering operation normally serves. Catering operations usually allow the guest to formulate the menu, but most caterers have a list of suggestions ready for guests who would like a little help in menu planning. This worksheet calculates a forecast for each of its suggested entrées when the expected customer count has been determined. It takes no more effort for the computer to forecast for all of the suggested entrées than to forecast the one entrée to be served, so the spreadsheet can be used for all of them.

After recording the menu items and their respective portion sizes, the first column requiring calculations is column D. Those entrées forecasted in terms of servings are represented by simply reentering the customer count in the proper cell. For example, cells D6, D7, D14, D15, and D16 all contain the formula +D3. Those forecasts resulting in AS pounds contain formulas that multiply portion size in ounces times the expected customer count, divided by 16 to convert the forecasts to AS pounds. For example, cell D8 contains the formula 10*D3/16. Since cell D27 results in gallons, its projection is divided by 128 rather than by 16.

Even though the projections have been made in column D, conversion to more useful forms is necessary in most cases. The following gives some explanation of the formulas used in column F. Although steak and chop portion sizes are usually in AP terms, the portion sizes of filets, New York strips, and pork chops are listed in AS terms for the student's practice in conversion to AP.

Cell	Menu Item	Formula	Explanation
F6	Beef S.-F.	(D6/35)+1	35 = recipe yield
F7	Beef strog.	(D7/20)+1	20 = recipe yield
F8	Filet mignon	(D8/.85)+1	AP yield = 85%
F9	N.Y. strip	(D9/.82)+1	AP yield = 82%
F10	Prime rib	(D10/.72)+1	AP yield = 72%
F11	Roast beef	(D11/.70)+1	AP yield = 70%
F12	Pork chops	(D12/.70)+1	AP yield = 70%
F13	Pork loin	(D13/.65)+1	AP yield = 65%
F14	S. S. pork	(D14/25)+1	25 = recipe yield
F15	Chix C. B.	(D15/96)+1	96 S per case
F16	Chix kiev	(D16/96)+1	96 S per case
F17	Chix S.-F.	(D17/15)+1	15 = recipe yield
F18	Fried chix	(D18/4)+1	4 quarters per head
F19	Turk. divan	(D19/20)+1	20 = recipe yield
F20	Turk. & dress.	(D20/.92)+1	AP yield = 92%
F21	Salmon	(D21/.66)+1	AP yield = 66%
F22	Sole	(D22/.72)+1	AP yield = 72%
F23	Lobster tail	(D23/12)+1	12 S per case
F24	Shrimp D. J.	(D24/50)+1	50 = recipe yield
F25	Fettuccini	(D25/40)+1	40 = recipe yield
F26	Lasagna	(D26/48)+1	48 = recipe yield
F27	Spaghetti	(D27/2.5)+1	2.5 gal = recipe yield

With a worksheet like the one described, a manager can forecast for the catering operation in terms that will be useful by simply entering the forecasted customer counts.

Problems

Here is the menu for an upcoming wedding reception dinner:

Shrimp cocktail: 6 21/25 PDQ in each serving

Prime rib: 7-oz AS rib eye roll with the lip off

Baked potato: 80-count Idaho

Whole green beans almondine: 3 oz of whole, frozen green beans per serving

Bibb lettuce with raspberry vinaigrette: ½ head per serving

Champagne: 2 3-oz glasses per guest (each bottle is a fifth of a gallon)

The guaranteed number of guests is 375. You will prepare for 10% more, so your expected customer count is 413. Using the customer count times portion size technique, forecast your food needs for the following:

1. Shrimp by the pound

2. Prime rib by the AS pound

3. Baked potatoes by the case

4. Frozen whole green beans by the pound

5. Bibb lettuce by the head

6. Champagne by the bottle

9 *Forecasting with a Recipe Factor*

The portion of a food served to a guest is often hidden within a recipe and not readily available to the forecasting planner. For example, while it is easy to determine how much chicken stir-fry a guest is to be served, it is not as easy to determine how much pulled chicken meat the serving contains, and therefore how much the purchasing agent should buy, since this amount is concealed within the operation's chicken stir-fry recipe. It is not difficult, however, to calculate how many times the recipe must be increased or decreased to successfully feed the group, and with this information it is easy to figure out how much of an individual recipe ingredient is needed for the total as well.

KEY TERMS

Ingredient amount
Recipe factor
Standardized recipe

Recipe Factor

Many times, when formulating a food order, the portion size of the ingredient being forecasted will not be known. For example, if meat loaf is being served, one can easily decide how much finished meat loaf to give each guest, but if onions need to be ordered for that meat loaf one won't know how much onion each guest will consume. The portion size for onions is hidden within the recipe. The technique described here makes it possible to determine the amount of a recipe ingredient needed for serving the entire party without knowing how much of that ingredient each guest will eat. (*Note:* It is assumed in this workbook that all of an operation's recipes are **standardized,** i.e., that they have been tested and found consistent in flavor, appearance, and yield.)

To figure how much of a recipe ingredient will be needed to feed an entire party, first calculate how many times that recipe will be used. The number of times that the recipe is increased or decreased is called the **recipe factor.** It can be found by dividing the forecasted customer count by the recipe yield in customers:

$$\text{Recipe factor} = \frac{\text{forecasted customer count}}{\text{recipe yield in customers}}$$

Here are a few examples:

1. You are feeding 200 people, and the recipe serves 25 guests.

$$\frac{200 \text{ people}}{\text{party}} \times \frac{1 \text{ recipe}}{25 \text{ people}} = \frac{8 \text{ recipes}}{\text{party}}$$

You will need to use a recipe factor of 8. (*Note:* It won't hurt to make nine recipes. Don't make seven, though, or the party may be short.)

2. You are expecting 300 guests, and the recipe makes 35 servings.

$$\frac{300 \text{ people}}{\text{party}} \times \frac{1 \text{ recipe}}{35 \text{ people}} = \frac{8.571 \text{ recipes}}{\text{party}}$$

Call that a recipe factor of 9. (*Note:* Be sure that you are using standardized recipes with yields that you can depend on.)

3. You are going to feed 40 people, and each recipe yields 100.

$$\frac{40 \text{ people}}{\text{party}} \times \frac{1 \text{ recipe}}{100 \text{ people}} = \frac{0.4 \text{ recipes}}{\text{party}}$$

You would probably use a recipe factor of 0.5. (*Note:* If you need to round off a calculated recipe factor, always round up.)

Forecasting with a Recipe Factor

Once the recipe factor has been calculated, multiply it times the **ingredient amount** used in that recipe. For example, if 1.5 lb of Bermudas are needed for each meat loaf recipe and there is a recipe and factor of 4 for the party, order at least 6 lb of onions:

$$\frac{4 \text{ recipes}}{\text{party}} \times \frac{1.5 \text{ lb onions}}{\text{recipe}} = \frac{6 \text{ lb onions}}{\text{party}}$$

Or if the recipe factor is 30, and the recipe calls for 4 tsp of salt:

$$\frac{30 \text{ recipes}}{\text{party}} \times \frac{4 \text{ tsp}}{\text{recipe}} = \frac{120 \text{ tsp}}{\text{party}}$$

(*Note:* To increase a recipe or baker's formula, do the arithmetic as shown for any ingredient, but be careful when adding things like baking soda, yeast, and spices. These things do not convert exactly, so add leaveners with care and add spices to taste. Use ingredient increases from a recipe factor for formulating purchases and recipe costing.)

▓▓▓▓ EXAMPLE

CHOPPED STEAK   YIELD: 30 S

Ground beef	10 lb
Onions, minced	12 oz
Salt	1 Tbsp
White pepper	1 tsp
Worchestershire	¼ cup

Using the recipe above, how much ground beef would you need to feed 175 people?

Solution

$$\underset{\substack{Customer \\ Count}}{\frac{175 \text{ people}}{\text{party}}} \times \underset{\substack{Recipe \\ Yield}}{\frac{1 \text{ recipe}}{30 \text{ people}}} = 5.833, \text{ or } \frac{6 \text{ recipes}}{\text{party}}$$

Then:

$$\underset{\substack{Recipe \\ Factor}}{\frac{6 \text{ recipes}}{\text{party}}} \times \underset{\substack{Ingredient \\ Amount}}{\frac{10 \text{ lb ground}}{\text{recipe}}} = \frac{60 \text{ lb ground beef}}{\text{party}}$$

The problem could also have been solved straight through like this:

$$\frac{175 \text{ people}}{\text{party}} \times \frac{\text{recipe}}{30 \text{ people}} \times \frac{10 \text{ lb ground}}{\text{recipe}} = \frac{58.333 \text{ lb ground}}{\text{party}}$$

(*Note:* Doing a problem straight through like this often creates an unwieldy recipe factor. It works fine mathematically, but for production purposes it is usually better to find the recipe factor first and then round it, if necessary, before continuing with the increase or decrease of the individual ingredient amounts.)

▓▓▓▓ EXAMPLE

How many onions would you need to feed 400 people the chopped steak recipe?

Solution

$$\underset{\substack{Customer \\ Count}}{\frac{400 \text{ people}}{\text{party}}} \times \underset{\substack{Recipe \\ Yield}}{\frac{1 \text{ recipe}}{30 \text{ people}}} = 13.333, \text{ or } \frac{14 \text{ recipes}}{\text{party}}$$

$$\underset{\substack{Recipe \\ Factor}}{\frac{14 \text{ recipes}}{\text{party}}} \times \underset{\substack{Ingredient \\ Amount}}{\frac{12 \text{ oz}}{1 \text{ recipe}}} = \frac{168 \text{ oz onions}}{\text{party}}$$

████████ **EXAMPLE**

To feed 340 people this recipe, how much would the Worchestershire cost if it costs $6.52 per gal?

Solution

$$\frac{340 \text{ people}}{\text{party}} \times \frac{1 \text{ recipe}}{30 \text{ people}} = 11.333, \text{ or } \frac{12 \text{ recipes}}{\text{party}}$$

$$\frac{12 \text{ recipes}}{\text{party}} \times \frac{.25 \text{ C}}{\text{recipe}} \times \frac{1 \text{ qt}}{4 \text{ cups}} \times \frac{1 \text{ gal}}{4 \text{ qt}} \times \frac{\$6.52}{\text{gal}} = 1.223 \text{ or about } \frac{\$1.22}{\text{party}}$$

This tool is useful in any menu situation that involves forecasting recipe ingredients from an estimated customer count. (*Note:* Like other forecasting methods, this one may work for all types of food and menu situations, but it's best to reserve its use for the more costly ingredients. Many ingredients are kept on hand in sufficient quantities so as to meet daily requirements.)

Computerizing Forecasting with a Recipe Factor

Forecasting with a recipe factor poses some new problems. There are millions of commonly used recipe ingredients, and many come in units unique to that ingredient. For example, parsley comes in bunches, cauliflower in heads, meat in pounds and ounces, and canned goods in ounces of weight or volume. Not only are these products described in these unique terms, they may also be costed out using a different label altogether.

Dealing with all of these possibilities is likely to be beyond the capabilities of most, if not all, spreadsheets. The manager who sets up a spreadsheet is not going to be able to foresee enough of these variations to make the worksheet of much generic use, since each spreadsheet will probably be specific to each recipe in the file. That is not a very practical solution for dealing with recipes. Fortunately, there are commercial packages on the market that the manager can use to cost and forecast any recipe. Every foodservice should own and use one of these programs. Comprehensive foodservice packages are expensive and may not be applicable in many operations, but recipe packages are different.

These programs account for most of the ways ingredients are described and priced. They allow the manager to change the portion size and therefore the customer yield of a recipe. They may also allow a manager to maintain a central price list that will then serve as the automatic price source for all recipe ingredients, rather than require prices to be updated on each recipe individually. Some even have the capability of obtaining prices from the data generated as invoices are checked at each delivery. Recipe costing is vital to a foodservice, but it is often not kept up to date because doing so is so time consuming. When a manager uses one of these programs recipe costing is not time consuming. Most of these programs can be used by the manager immediately, and they are no more expensive than a common spreadsheet program. Therefore, it is the author's recommendation that a manager make use of one of these computerized recipe packages for his or her recipe forecasting instead of trying to program a spreadsheet to do the same thing.

Problems

CHICKEN STIR-FRY   **YIELD: 15 S**

Chicken breast, cut in ¼-inch strips	4 lb
Snow peas	2 lb
Carrots, julienne	2.5 lb
Water chestnuts, sliced	12 oz
Almonds, whole, blanched	10 oz
Broccoli buds	1.5 lb
Green onions, sliced	4 each
Soy sauce	3 oz
Honey	3 oz
Chicken stock	3 cups
Sherry	4 oz
Corn starch	2 oz

Based on the recipe above, forecast for the following ingredients, given the expected customer counts. (*Note:* To check answers against those in the back of the book, round any recipe factor that doesn't come out even up to the next half recipe. A recipe factor of 2.3 would be a factor of 2.5.)

1. Snow peas for a party of 80.

2. Pounds of bone-in, raw chicken breast for 325 people, given a 40% loss to trim and bones to get the strips needed.

3. Pounds of whole, blanched almonds for a party of 130.

4. Pounds of whole carrots for the julienne carrots called for in the recipe, given a 17% peel and cutting loss from AP to julienne strips, for a party of 225.

5. Pounds of AP broccoli, given a 62% trim loss from AP to buds, for 45 people.

6. Ounces of soy sauce for 450 people.

Chapter **10** *Piece Yield*

OVERVIEW

With long experience and familiarity with a product, one can learn how many portions can be expected from a given quantity, such as a cut of meat or a case of produce. This amount of yielded portions is not obtained from books or from product statistical data, but is dependent on the business's portion size offered to its guests. When, through experience, a purchasing agent has gained this knowledge, he or she can use it as an effective tool to forecast needed supplies in any menu situation.

KEY TERM

Piece yield

Piece Yield

A simple method of forecasting from a customer count is to know how many servings one can expect from a quantity such as a case of food or a cut of meat. The number of servings obtained from a given quantity of food is called that quantity's **piece yield.** If, for example, experience has taught that 100 salads can be made from a case of lettuce, it's easy to use the information to determine that four cases will be needed to feed 400 people. To forecast food needs from an expected customer count, divide that customer count by the piece yield of the food being considered:

$$\text{Forecast} = \frac{\text{customer count}}{\text{piece yield}}$$

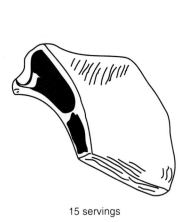

15 servings

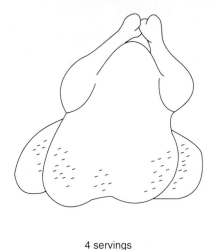

4 servings

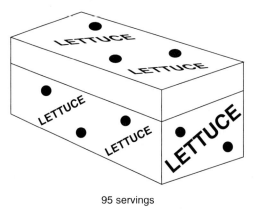

95 servings

Piece Yield

▓▓▓▓ **EXAMPLE**

How many top butts will it take to serve a party of 324 if you usually get 17 servings from a butt?

Solution

$$324 \text{ servings} \times \frac{1 \text{ top butt}}{17 \text{ servings}} = 19.059, \text{ or about 20 top butts}$$

This method is quick and reasonably accurate, but it is definitely not recommended for the beginning purchaser. It takes considerable time on the job to know how many servings come from any particular market form of food product. And, before any purchasing agent can use this method of forecasting, he or she must have developed considerable product yield knowledge.

When using this tool, be careful to include size ranges in purchase specifications to purveyors. Not all cases or cuts of meat are the same size, so it is important to include an acceptable weight range when ordering a cut of meat and planning to forecast this way. It should also be noted that, in planning, the forecast depends on a fixed portion size; that is, if the piece yield is 15 3-oz servings, the same piece yield will not hold for a 5.5-oz portion size.

Note that, when using this method of forecasting, the final figure will nearly always be AP. This is because an estimate of AS servings obtainable from an AP case or cut of meat has the waste built into it. It will therefore seldom be necessary to convert this type of forecast to AP before ordering.

Computerizing Forecasting with a Piece Yield

Like the customer count times portion size worksheet, the piece yield worksheet is more useful as a record than as an aid to calculations. Forecasting with a piece yield requires few calculations, but the spreadsheet is a logical place to record purchasing specifications. (See the sample worksheet below.)

Unless the same market form of the commodity used is purchased time after time, piece yield estimates are not reliable. For example, the piece yield for inside round will not be consistent if the rounds purchased are of different quality and size each time they are purchased. The worksheet is an excellent place for these purchasing specifications to be recorded. The author has included some of this information on the worksheet—approximate size of the market forms to be purchased, for instance—but has left much of what may be recorded on this sheet to the student's imagination. The business may wish to record such purchasing characteristics as IMPS numbers for meat cuts, acceptable weight ranges, quality grades, and preferred market forms.

The sample worksheet should show all of the commodities for which the manager has formulated a piece yield. Since piece yield forecasts are so simple, the worksheet forecasts for all commodities and lets the manager use the ones desired. Only column F contains any calculations: cell F6 = (D3/E6)+1, cell F7 = (D3/E7)+1, and cell F8 = (D3/E8)+1, and so on. With a worksheet like this a manager can maintain purchasing specifications and make piece yield (P Yield) forecasts simply by entering the forecasted customer counts.

	A	B	C	D	E	F	G
1	**Piece Yield Worksheet**						
2							
3	Forecasted Customer Count			525			
4							
5	MEAT		Size	Portion	P Yield	Forecast	
6	C B brisket		9 lb	5 oz	14	38	
7	Ham		12 lb	7 oz	24	22	
8	Inside		20 lb	7 oz	32	17	
9	Pork loin		10 lb	7 oz	15	36	
10	#109 rib		18 lb	12 oz	15	36	
11	Strip loin		15 lb	12 oz	16	33	
12	Tenderloin		8 lb	8 oz	14	38	
13	Top butt		10 lb	7 oz	17	31	
14	Turkey brt		10 lb	5 oz	30	18	
15							
16	DAIRY						
17	Bleu wheel		6 lb	1 oz	90	6	
18	Brie wheel		2 kg	1 oz	65	9	
19	Milk		6 gal	8 oz	96	6	
20	Ice cream		3 gal	#12 scoop	70	8	
21							
22	VEGETABLES						
23	Broccoli		1 case	4 oz	48	11	
24	Carrots		50 lb	4 oz	140	4	
25	Cauliflower		1 case	4 oz	72	8	
26	Lettuce		1 case	3 oz	100	6	
27	Romaine		1 case	3 oz	75	8	
28							
29							

Problems

1. How many inside rounds will you need to feed 340 people if the piece yield on an inside is 55 servings?

2. How many #10 cans of sliced peaches will you need to feed 85 people if the piece yield is 24 servings per #10 can?

3. How many cases of iceberg lettuce will you need to feed 480 people if the piece yield on lettuce is 95 servings per case?

4. How many pounds of coffee will you need in order to give 800 people 2 cups of coffee each if a pound of coffee has a piece yield of 64 cups per pound of dry grounds?

5. How many gallons of syrup will you need to give 340 children 10 oz of orange drink if a gallon of syrup has a piece yield of 100 10-oz servings per gallon?

6. How many boxes of bulk potato chips will you need to feed 280 people 2 oz each if a box of chips has a piece yield of 24 2-oz servings?

Summary of Forecasting Techniques

This concludes the information on forecasting methods as they apply to the different types of menus. In summary, use the forecasting tools as follows:

1. Sales menu
   a. Daily usage par
   b. Recipe factor × ingredient amount
   c. Customer count ÷ piece yield
2. Equal cycle menu
   a. Forecast similar to previous history
   b. Recipe factor × ingredient amount
   c. Customer count ÷ piece yield
3. Long cycle menu
   a. Usage ratio
   b. Recipe factor × ingredient amount
   c. Customer count ÷ piece yield
4. Special event menu
   a. Customer count × portion size
   b. Recipe factor × ingredient amount
   c. Customer count ÷ piece yield

   As you gain experience you may run across even better forecasting tools than these; but as a beginner these will be useful in almost any menu situation.

PART III Adjustments

Chapter 11 AS to AP Conversion

As discussed in Chapter 4, the AS/AP conversion formula is the recommended method for adjusting AS estimates to AP needs. Sometimes, however, waste percentages are not available to the purchasing agent. Although they can always be determined experimentally, it is often better for the planner to formulate a more versatile tool, the yield analysis factor (YAF). One can often choose between several products that will adequately fill the need, and the YAF will point out the least expensive one. It can also be used to convert AS amounts to AP requirements.

KEY TERM

Yield analysis factor

Throughout the forecasting process, it is important to keep track of a food's state of refinement. If a forecast yields an amount in AS terms, it will often be necessary to convert it to an AP figure before ordering. If purchases require the conversion between AS and AP, this can easily be done with the yield formula:

$$AP = \frac{AS \times 100}{100 - W}$$

Computerizing Yield Formula Calculations

As an alternative to piece yield calculations, the manager may wish to convert AS projected forecasts to AP quantities with the yield formula. Like several other techniques discussed in this workbook, yield calculations are simple and need not be computerized, but a spreadsheet set up for such conversion is also an excellent place to store purchasing specification data and waste percentages. A suggestion for a yield formula (AS/AP) worksheet is shown below.

Notice that the yield formula has been used in two different forms:

$$\frac{AS \times 100\%}{100\% - W\%} \quad \text{and} \quad \frac{AS}{Yield}$$

The first uses waste percentage as a whole number, and the second calls on the programmer to convert waste to yield in decimal terms. A conversion for inside rounds would look like this:

$$\frac{107 \times 100}{100 - 30} \quad \text{or} \quad \frac{107}{0.70}$$

The first formula, while appearing to be the more complex of the two, is more easily used mentally, while the second takes up less room in a computer program.

The only calculations required on this sheet are in column E. Cell E6 contains the formula C3*100/(100 D6)+1. As mentioned above, the formula could have been shortened considerably if the yield in decimal terms had been recorded in column D instead of waste in percentage terms. Either form is equally effective. Whichever form is preferred, one needs only to record the AS needs.

	A	B	C	D	E
1	**AS/AP Worksheet**				
2					
3		EP Weight	217 lb		
4					
5	Commodity	USDA Qual	Size/Pack	Waste %	AP Weight
6	Inside	Choice	20 lb each	30	311
7	Steamship	Choice	55 lb each	42	375
8	Top butt	Choice	15 lb each	26	294
9	109 rib	Choice	18 lb each	34	329
10	Strip loin	Choice	15 lb each	27	298
11	Pork loin	#1	12 lb each	31	315
12	Ham, Bl	Debuke F	15 lb each	18	265
13	Chicken	A	3 lb each	51	443
14	Turkey	A	18 lb each	48	418
15	Broccoli	Fancy	12/case	41	368
16	Cauliflower	Fancy	12/case	37	345
17	Snow peas	Fancy	loose, lb	16	259
18	Asparagus	Fancy	24 bu/case	23	282
19	Bel carrot	Fancy	loose, lb	24	286
20	Temples	Fancy	88/case	63	587
21	Canteloupe	Fancy	24/case	46	402
22	Honey dew	Fancy	10/case	41	368
23	Watermelon	Fancy	20 lb each	37	345
24	Grapes	Fancy	28 lb/case	11	244
25	Kiwi	Fancy	24/case	14	253
26	Grapefruit	Fancy	45/case	32	320
27	Pineapple	Fancy	12/case	42	375
28					
29					

Yield Analysis Factor

The **yield analysis factor** (YAF) is a special technique that can be used to calculate AS/AP conversion for commonly used cuts of meat or for anything else that is expensive and has inherent waste. (*Note:* For use of this technique, it is assumed that the foodservice involved does not cut its own meats, but uses them as they come from the purveyor. When a business cuts its own meat, some trim has value and is usable in other products.) Once determined, the YAF can help pinpoint which cut of meat is the best buy on a given day, and then will convert AS needs to the AP amount needed to purchase. The YAF is determined by the following formula:

$$YAF = \frac{AP \text{ weight}}{AS \text{ weight}}$$

Since AP is 100% and AS = 100% – W%, the YAF is actually the circled portion of the yield formula:

$$AP = \frac{AS \times 100}{(100 - W)}$$

(*Note:* The more waste incurred during trimming, cooking, and portioning, the larger the YAF. An item with no waste, such as presliced bologna [AP and AS being the same], will have a YAF of 1.000. A cut of meat with a 50% waste factor will have a YAF of 2.000.)

The YAF is useful in most any foodservice. For example, when a party is to be served roast round of beef, a chef will have several options—inside round, outside round, or even gooseneck round. Properly handled, any of these cuts will yield an appealing dish for the guest, but each has its own waste factor and its own ever-changing AP price from the purveyor. The YAF can pinpoint which cut will provide the best buy on a given day, given these waste and price variables.

To determine the YAF, one must first experiment with the cuts of meat that are commonly used. This experimentation must be done carefully because the accuracy of the YAF will determine how effective purchasing becomes. Finding and using a YAF calls for real consistency in the way the staff handles meat. Meat handling procedures should be standardized so that the results of the YAF experimentation can be applied. Here are some standardized meat handling procedures:

1. Preheat the oven and roast at the same temperature each time that particular cut of meat is prepared.
2. Put the meat in the oven directly from the cooler so that it will always go into the oven at the same temperature.
3. Always use a meat thermometer to determine doneness. Cook to the same degree of internal doneness each time.
4. After cooking, allow all meat to rest outside the oven for the same length of time before slicing.
5. Use a sharp slicer.

Determining the YAF

It is important to use the same procedures in everyday meat handling that are used when determining the YAF. It is generally better to do YAF experiments with large amounts of meat. The larger the sample, the less effect individual piece characteristics will have on the results. For example, if a YAF was determined by testing only one piece of inside round, the result will be slanted if that particular piece is more or less lean than usual. Returning to the YAF formula, recall that

$$YAF = \frac{AP \text{ weight}}{AS \text{ weight}}$$

The AP weight is the easiest element to obtain. Just weigh all of the raw meat before trimming or cooking. If an entire delivery is used, this could be the amount on the invoice.

The AS amount is more difficult to determine. It can best be found using the following method:

1. Weigh the empty counter pans that the meat will be held in after portioning.
2. Roast, slice, portion, and pan the meat according to your standardized meat handling procedures.
3. Weigh the full counter pans of cooked, portioned meat.
4. Subtract the weight of the empty counter pans from the weight of the full pans. This is the AS weight of the meat.

After both of these quantities have been found, calculate the YAF for that cut of meat. For instance, here is an example of an experiment on inside round that was conducted as described above:

$$YAF = \frac{AP \text{ weight} = 174 \text{ lb}}{AS \text{ weight} = 122 \text{ lb}} = 1.426$$

This same procedure should then be followed for the other cuts of meat that are being considered for roast round of beef. When completed, there will be a YAF for each cut of meat that might be used. Here are the results of similar work on outside round and gooseneck round:

$$YAF = \frac{AP \text{ weight} = 97 \text{ lb}}{AS \text{ weight} = 61 \text{ lb}} = 1.590$$

$$YAF = \frac{AP \text{ weight} = 215 \text{ lb}}{AS \text{ weight} = 122 \text{ lb}} = 1.762$$

Now that the YAFs have been determined experimentally, one can be confident that future purchases will perform in much the same manner as those tested.

Using the YAF: Which Cut of Meat to Buy

One of the problems addressed by the YAF is that each cut of meat, with its own characteristic waste factor, also has a unique AP market price that fluc-

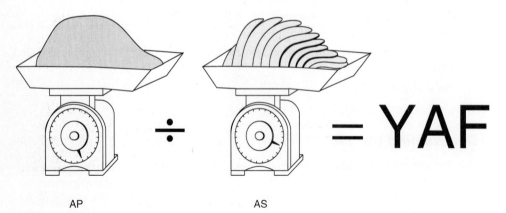

AP   AS

Yield Analysis Factor

tuates almost daily. To determine the best buy, look for the lowest price for an AS pound of meat. To determine which cut of meat offers the lowest cost per AS pound of meat, use the following formula:

$$\text{AS price per pound} = \text{AP price per pound} \times \text{YAF}$$

In other words, by multiplying the current market AP price per pound by the corresponding YAF, one will find the cost of an AS pound of that meat (i.e., the cost of a cooked, trimmed, portioned pound of that meat with the waste taken into account).

▓▓▓▓ EXAMPLE

If the current prices for AP beef round are as follows, which will be the best buy given the YAFs noted above?

Cut	AP price
Inside	$2.65/lb
Outside	$2.41/lb
Gooseneck	$2.22/lb

Solution

Cut	AP price	×	YAF	=	AS price
Inside	$2.65/lb	×	1.426	=	$3.78/lb
Outside	$2.41/lb	×	1.590	=	$3.83/lb
Gooseneck	$2.22/lb	×	1.762	=	$3.91/lb

At $3.78/lb, inside round will be the least expensive as a finished product, even though it has the highest AP price per pound.

Note that the AS price that results from the above YAF operation is a food cost consideration only, and does not consider the added labor required to portion more of a wastier, although less costly, cut of meat. While trimming, slicing, and portioning during the YAF test, figure out how much it costs in labor to portion a pound of each AP cut. The combined food *and* labor information would point to the best value of the day.

Using the YAF: How Much to Buy

Now that it has been determined which cut would be the most economical to purchase, one can calculate how much of that cut to buy. Using one of the previously given forecasting tools, such as customer count times portion size, determine how much AS meat is needed, and from this calculate how much AP to purchase using the following formula:

$$\text{AP weight} = \text{AS weight} \times \text{YAF}$$

The expected AS needs of the party times the YAF of the chosen cut will tell how much AP to order. For instance, it has been determined that inside rounds will be purchased for the party. As previously determined, insides have a YAF of 1.426. Since 375 people are expected, and a 4-oz AS portion will be provided, the total AS estimate is as follows:

$$\frac{375 \text{ people}}{\text{party}} \times \frac{4 \text{ oz}}{\text{person}} \times \frac{1 \text{ lb}}{16 \text{ oz}} = 93.75, \text{ or about 94 lb AS}$$

To get an AP estimate for the party, multiply by the YAF:

$$94 \text{ lb} \times 1.426 = 134.044, \text{ or about 135 lb of AP insides}$$

Computerizing YAF Calculations

YAF calculations are done easily with a spreadsheet program. Page 91 contains a sample worksheet that includes both the YAF-derived AS cost and the probable labor cost of processing that particular selection. The combination of these two factors should give an accurate picture of the costs involved so the manager can make a good selection.

As in manual calculations, cell C3 and column B represent the data the program needs initially. These items can be input whenever the manager needs to consult the YAF projections. From the AP price per pound and the YAF, the price per AS pound can be calculated and placed in column D. The formula in cell D6 is B6*C6, and the others in column D are similar.

To determine the labor cost, keep track of the hours of labor required to portion a cooked piece of meat and then divide that time by the original piece's weight. This will result in the labor cost needed to portion an AP pound of that cut.

To calculate total labor estimates, the needed AP weight must be known. That is found by multiplying the forecasted AS weight by the cut's YAF, and is recorded in column F; for example, cell F6 contains the formula C3*C6. Following this calculation, total labor estimates can be recorded in column H; for example, cell H6 contains the formula E6*F6. In making these estimates, the manager must be careful to use the AP weight, not the AS forecast.

The total AS cost, found in column G of the worksheet, is the most important factor in these estimates. This cost estimate can be calculated in either of two ways: AS price per pound times the AS weight needed, or AP price per pound times the AP weight needed.

Finally, food and labor costs are put together. This gives a manager a complete picture of the upcoming expense on which to base the purchasing decisions. Cell I6 contains the formula G6+H6. Therefore, the manager can project future expenditures by simply updating AP prices and the estimated AS weight to be used.

YAF Worksheet

	A	B	C	D	E	F	G	H	I
1	**YAF Worksheet**								
2									
3	AS Weight		427						
4									
5	Beef	Price/AP lb	YAF	Price/AS lb	Labor/AP lb	AP Weight	AS Cost	Labor Cost	Total Cost
6	Gooseneck	$2.37	1.666	$3.94	$0.15	712	$1682.38	$106.80	$1789.18
7	Inside	$2.78	1.428	$3.96	$0.12	610	$1690.92	$73.20	$1764.12
8	Outside	$2.54	1.538	$3.90	$0.13	657	$1665.30	$85.41	$1750.71
9									
10	CB Brisket								
11	Ckd D off	$2.63	1.111	$2.92	$0.12	475	$1246.84	$57.00	$1303.84
12	Raw D on	$1.79	2.000	$3.58	$0.21	855	$1528.66	$179.55	$1708.21
13									
14	Ham								
15	Ckd bnls	$2.66	1.086	$2.88	$0.11	464	$1229.76	$51.04	$1280.80
16	Raw B in	$1.95	1.612	$3.14	$0.16	689	$1340.78	$110.24	$1451.02
17									
18	Pork								
19	BRT loin	$2.42	1.538	$3.72	$0.13	657	$1588.44	$85.41	$1673.85
20	Can back	$2.56	1.449	$3.70	$0.12	619	$1579.90	$74.28	$1654.18
21									
22	Turkey								
23	Ckd bnls	$2.15	1.098	$2.36	$0.10	469	$1007.72	$46.90	$1054.62
24	Raw B in	$1.63	1.960	$3.19	$0.22	837	$1362.13	$184.14	$1546.27
25									
26									
27									
28									
29									

Problems

Your catering business has conducted yield experiments on the following cuts of meat:

Cut	Weight AP	Weight AS
Beef inside round	318 lb	223 lb
Turkey breast, raw, bone-in	158 lb	87 lb
Roast BRT pork loin	217 lb	128 lb
Beef outside round	146 lb	93 lb
Boneless, cooked ham	174 lb	155 lb
Raw, whole corned beef brisket	184 lb	92 lb
Cooked corned beef brisket, deckle off	256 lb	208 lb
Roast pork, Canadian back	117 lb	74 lb
Turkey breast, raw, boneless	184 lb	142 lb
Bone-in, uncooked ham	246 lb	150 lb

Calculate the YAFs for:

1. Inside round

2. Outside round

3. Raw, bone-in turkey breast

4. Raw, boneless turkey breast

5. BRT pork loin

6. Canadian back

7. Raw, whole corned beef brisket

8. Cooked corned beef brisket, deckle off

9. Cooked, boneless ham

10. Uncooked, bone-in ham

With YAFs in hand, you're ready to start getting a better value for your purchasing dollar. The following is your purveyor's price list for the week:

Item	AP Price
Inside round	$2.86
Outside round	$2.63
Hot dog, all beef, 8/1	$1.74
BRT pork loin	$2.91
BRT fresh ham	$1.86
Canadian back	$2.83
Imported picnic, 4 × 4	$1.61
Ham, uncooked, bone-in	$1.33
Ham, cooked, boneless	$2.08
Bacon, hotel, 18–22	$2.11
Turkey breast, raw, bone-in	$1.02
Turkey breast, ckd. boneless	$2.63
Turkey breast, raw, boneless	$1.87
Corned beef brisket, whole, raw	$1.51
Corned beef brisket, ckd., D.O.	$2.37
Beef tenderloin, PSMO	$6.41
N.Y. strip, 14 oz	$5.63
Beef rib, IMPS #109	$4.31
Beef rib, IMPS #110	$4.63

Forecast for the week's parties:

a. Which will be the most economical cuts of meat to buy? Use your calculated YAFs and the above prices. You do not need to consider labor costs.

b. Calculate the AP amounts that you will need to buy.

c. Determine the purchase cost for the amount needed for each party.

	Entrée	Portion Size	Forecasted Customer Count
1.	Roast beef	6 oz/S	380
2.	Turkey & dressing	5 oz/S	215
3.	Roast beef	6 oz/S	310
4.	Corned beef & cabbage	5 oz/S	155

5.   Baked ham   7 oz/S   250

6.   Roast pork   6 oz/S   325

Chapter 12 Adjustments to Forecasts

OVERVIEW

Many forecasts are labeled in units that are unacceptable to the purveyor. Initial forecasts are often made in ounces, but it is usually necessary to convert them into units such as pounds or gallons. It is also desirable to look ahead and see if any commodities need to be purchased earlier than usual for prepreparation. Before ordering, usable inventory must be deducted from any estimate to avoid ordering more than is needed. Finally, needs for some items must be expressed in full cases, since partial cases are often not available for purchase.

KEY TERMS

Case size

Mise en place

Usable units

Adjustment to Usable Units

Forecasting calculations often result in ounces, the measure often used in portion size. If this is the case, these estimates need to be converted to **usable units** such as gallons, pounds, or some other measure that is easier to communicate to a purveyor. This conversion is usually done during or immediately after formulating the AS estimate. (Conversion is discussed in the Appendix.)

Adjustment for Mise en Place

Mise en place refers to prepreparation, or work done ahead of time. To understand this idea, refer to the following ordering pattern:

97

	Mon.	Tue.	Wed.	Thu.	Fri.	Sat.	Sun.	Mon.	Tue.
Order 1	ord.	del.	use	use	use			ord.	del.
Order 2				ord.	del.	use	use	use	use

Note that there are Monday and Thursday orders for Tuesday and Friday deliveries. Assume that a restaurant is going to serve breaded ocean perch fillets on Sunday, and that they prefer to buy unbreaded fillets and do the breading themselves. If the fish will be served on Sunday, it should be breaded on Saturday, and this probably means it should begin thawing out as early as Thursday. Thus, because of mise en place requirements, the fillets should be ordered on Monday rather than on Thursday. In general, anything frozen that must be thawed and then preprepped, or foods that need to be marinated or soaked, might require advanced delivery.

Adjustment for Usable Inventory

As illustrated in the discussion of par forecasting, forecasted estimates are not necessarily the amount that will be purchased. It is safe to think of any forecasted estimate, regardless of how it was formulated, as a build-to. Adjust what is needed by the amount on hand and purchase the difference, but be careful to adjust low-level pars for inventory and daily usage pars for usable inventory.

Adjustment for Case Size

Often a purveyor will not break up a case and sell only part of it. In such instances, a whole case must be purchased even if only one can is needed. Different **case sizes** are used for various food products; for example, #10 cans come six to the case, 46-oz soup concentrate and juice cans come twelve to the case, and gallons usually come four or six to the case.

This concludes the discussion of adjustments to forecasts. Each of these tools presented, or a combination of them, can be very useful in certain purchasing or production situations.

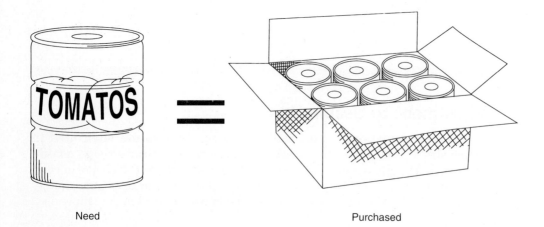

Need   Purchased

Adjustment for Case Size

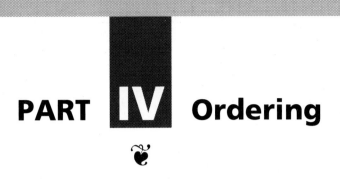

PART **IV** Ordering

Chapter ▮13▮ *Forecasting/Ordering Exercise*

OVERVIEW

This chapter includes all of the material needed to complete a relatively comprehensive purchasing problem. Given menus, recipes, forecasted customer counts, usage history, price bids, YAFs, and inventory information, the student will forecast for a hypothetical in-plant feeder and make the proper adjustments to convert those forecasts into an order.

The following problem is intended to be realistic and very similar to what a manager will encounter when actually purchasing. In fact, it probably calls on the student to be a little more careful and accurate than in an actual purchasing situation. In actual purchasing, some shortcuts would probably be used. The methods presented in this workbook and used in this problem, although quite accurate, may be more time consuming than is necessary in actual purchasing situations. However, they provide safe ordering procedures for the beginning purchaser who has not yet learned where to take shortcuts, and they provide safe ordering procedures for the more experienced purchaser whose shortcuts have resulted in food cost problems.

To put together a food order, many different kinds of information may be needed:

1. Par information
2. YAFs
3. Usage ratios
4. Recipes
5. Menus
6. Purchase prices
7. Ordering patterns

Forecasting/Ordering Problem

You are purchasing for a lunch only, five-day-per-week, in-plant foodservice operation. We will simplify the ordering process by assuming that you buy everything from one purveyor and therefore have to place only one order. The following is your order schedule for the portion of the cycle you will need to use:

Week one of cycle					Week two of cycle				
Mon.	Tues.	Wed.	Thu.	Fri.	Mon.	Tues.	Wed.	Thu.	Fri.
ord.	del.	use	use	use	ord.	del.	use	use	use
			ord.	del.	use	use			

You are going to formulate an order to be used on Wednesday, Thursday, and Friday. You will call in the order Monday after lunch, and it should be delivered sometime on Tuesday. Your operation includes three types of menus:

1. A sales menu for a grill operation that offers:

    Hamburgers, 4/1, 80/20 ground beef

    Italian beef, 3.5 oz/S, from some kind of round

    Hot dogs, 8/1, all beef

    Chili, 13 8-oz servings per #10 can

    French fries, 3.5 oz/S, 27 lb per case

    Grilled cheese, 2 slices of American cheese per sandwich

2. A special event menu that caters to special functions. This week you have three parties:

    a. Monday—15 people
    Shrimp Newburg on puff pastry
    Fruit platter

    b. Wednesday—36 people
    Beef tornedo, 2 3-oz AP tenderloin per serving
    Snow peas, 2 oz AS/S, 3% W AP to AS
    Julienne carrots, 2 oz AS/S, 8% W from AP
    Crème caramel

    c. Thursday—26 people
    Boneless chicken breast, 8 oz AP/S on wild rice
    Broccoli buds, 3 oz AS/S, 66% W from AP
    Three-chocolate cheesecake, 16 S/cake, 4 cakes/case

3. A cycle menu for your cafeteria line. Here is the part of it that you'll need to order from. Included are your forecasted customer counts and previous usage ratios. This cycle is an equal cycle, so the next time through, Monday #1 will fall on a Monday again.

Menu Item	Forecasted Customer Count	Previous Usage Ratio
Monday Week 1	420	
Liver & onions, 4/1 calves liver		0.248 S/C
Pork chops, 3/1 center cut chops		0.417 S/C
Cheese ravioli, frozen		0.023 S/C
Tuesday Week 1	455	
Turkey & dress., 3-oz ckd. breast		0.349 S/C
Lasagna, frozen		0.319 S/C
Fish & Chips, 4 oz/S, from cod fillets		0.156 S/C
Wednesday Week 1	430	
Beef round, 7 oz AS/S		0.246 lb/C
Pork fried rice, ½″ pork stew, recipe		0.208 S/C
Salmon croquettes, from recipe		0.135 S/C
Thursday Week 1	450	
Fried chicken, 2½ lb/hd, ¼ chix/S		0.183 hd./C
Spaghetti with meat sauce, recipe		0.181 S/C
Ham and au gratin potatoes, recipe		0.063 S/C
Friday Week 1	435	
Chopped steak, recipe		0.316 S/C
Chicken stir-fry, recipe		0.252 S/C
BBQ beef sandwich, on a kaiser roll, 3.5 oz AS/S, round		0.106 lb/C
Monday Week 2	415	
Baked haddock, 4 oz AP/S		0.131 lb/C
Sauerbraten, 7 oz AS/S, round		0.216 lb/C
Italian sausage, 4/1, French bread		0.311 S/C
Tuesday Week 2	450	
Sweet & sour pork, ½″ pork stew		0.064 lb/C
Creamed chipped beef on baker, 6 oz SOS/S		0.045 S/C
French fried shrimp, 6 21/25 /S		0.371 lb/C
Wednesday Week 2	440	
Honey-baked chicken, 2½ lb/hd, ¼ chix/S		0.246 hd./C
Beef stew, 8 oz/S, recipe		0.189 S/C
American goulash, 7 oz/S, recipe		0.092 S/C

The recipes you'll need are as follows. (To match the answers in the back of the book, round *all* calculated recipe factors up to the next ½ recipe.)

MEAT SAUCE   YIELD: 75 S

Spaghetti sauce	4 #10 cans
Ground beef	10 lb AP
Fennel	¼ cup
Oregano	2 Tbsp
Basil	2 Tbsp
Garlic salt	2 Tbsp

CHOPPED STEAK   YIELD: 30 S

Ground beef	10 lb AP
Onions, chopped	1½ lb
Worchestershire sauce	½ cup

HAM & AU GRATIN POTATOES   YIELD: 50 S

Ham, ckd, diced, ½″	6 lb AS
Potatoes, sliced	10 lb
Onions, sliced	2 lb
Milk	3 qt.
Roux	¾ cup
Salt	to taste
Pepper, white	to taste
Mustard, dry	to taste
Worchestershire sauce	¼ cup
Cheddar cheese, sharp	1¾ lb

CHICKEN STIR-FRY   YIELD: 15 S

Chicken breast, bnls	4 lb AP
Snow peas, 3% W	2 lb AS
Julienne carrots, 8% W	2½ lb AS
Water chestnuts, sliced	12 oz
Almonds, whole	10 oz
Broccoli, buds, 66% W	1½ lb AS
Green onions, sliced	4 each
Soy sauce	3 oz
Honey	3 oz
Sherry	4 oz
Chicken stock	3 cups
Cornstarch	2 oz
Oil	½ cup

PORK FRIED RICE   YIELD: 40 S

Pork stew, ½″	7 lb AP
Rice, cooked	6 qt
BBQ sauce	¼ cup
Eggs, AA, large	8 each
Snow peas, 3% W	2 lb AS
Green onions, sliced	1 bunch
Soy sauce	½ cup
Oil	½ cup

YAFs as previously determined:

Meat Cut	YAF
Inside round	1.426
Outside round	1.570
Ham, unckd, bone-in	1.640
Ham, ckd, bnls	1.123
Pork loin, BRT	1.695
Canadian back	1.581
Turkey brst, raw, bone-in	1.816
Turkey brst, raw, bnls	1.296

The price list from your meat purveyor for the week is as follows:

Meat Cut	AP Cost
Inside round	$2.94/lb
109 rib	$4.38/lb
Hamburger, 80/20	$1.85/lb
Hot dog, 8/1, all beef, 10 lb/box	$1.63/lb
Outside round	$2.76/lb
Chicken brst, bnls, 48 S/case, 8 oz	$44.64/case
Tenderloin, PSMO	$6.56/lb
Ham, uncooked, bone-in	$1.63/lb
Ham, cooked, bnls	$2.10/lb
Pork loin, BRT	$2.87/lb
Canadian back	$2.71/lb
Bacon, 18–22, hotel	$2.13/lb
Shrimp, 21–25, PDQ, 3 lb/bag	$18.51/3 lb
Cod fillet	$1.49/lb
Pork stew, ½″	$1.65/lb
Haddock fillet	$1.89/lb
Beef patties, 4/1, 10 lb/box	$18.80/box

The following is the relevant par information:

1. Low-level par:

   Milk: 6 6-gal dispensers for the order period

   Chili: Chef Mate, 5 #10 cans for the order period

   French fries: shoestring, 27 lb/case, 4 cases for the order period

   American cheese: sliced, 3 lb/block, 4 blocks for the order period

   Carrots: 1 50-lb sack for the order period

   Lettuce: 24 head/case, 3 cases for the order period

2. Daily usage par:

   Hamburger patties: 25 lb/day

   Hamburger buns: 9 dozen/day

   Hot dogs: 8 lb/day

   Hot dog buns: 10 buns/package, 7 packages/day

   Round for Italian beef: 18 lb AS/day

On Monday afternoon, after the close of business, the following food is on hand:

Food Item	Amount
Carrots	10 lb
Beef inside round	25 lb AP
Chicken brst, bnls, 48 S/case, 8 oz	½ case
French fries, shoestring, 27 lb/case	2 cases
Hot dog buns, 10/package	9 packages
Chili, Chef Mate, #10	8 #10 cans
Hamburger buns, 12/package	8 packages
Hot dogs, all beef, 8/1	12 lb
Hamburger patties, 4/1	38 lb
American cheese, sliced, 3 lb/block	1 block
Hamburger, bulk, 80/20	10 lb
Milk, 6-gal dispenser	2 6 gal
Cod fillet, 5-lb box	3 5-lb boxes
Lettuce, 2 dozen/case	2 cases

Problems

Given the information, prepare the food order to be delivered on Tuesday of week #1, to be used on Wednesday, Thursday, and Friday of that week. You should be ready to call in the food order after the close of business on Monday for a Tuesday delivery. Formulate an order for the following:

1. Some kind of beef round for all of your round needs by the AP pound.
2. Hot dog buns by the 10-bun package.
3. Sliced American cheese by the 3-lb block.
4. Hamburger patties by the 10-lb box.
5. Bulk hamburger by the 10-lb bag.
6. Boneless chicken breast by the 48-S case.
7. Shoestring french fries by the 27-lb case.
8. Milk by the 6-gal dispenser.
9. All-beef, 8/1 hot dogs by the 10-lb box.
10. Chili by the #10 can.
11. PSMO tenderloin by the AP pound.
12. ½″ pork stew by the AP pound.
13. 2½-lb chickens, by the head, quartered.
14. Spaghetti sauce by the #10 can.
15. Hamburger buns by the 12-bun package.
16. Some kind of ham for the Ham & Au Gratin Potatoes recipe by the AP pound.
17. Carrots by the 50-lb sack.
18. Snow peas by the AP pound.
19. Lettuce by the 24-head case.
20. Broccoli by the AP pound.

Chapter 14 Calling in the Order

OVERVIEW

Once the forecasting and formulation of an order are complete, the order must be written down in a logical fashion and called in. The contents of the order and its expected date of arrival should then be available to the management personnel responsible for the different activities of the business.

KEY TERMS

Bid order sheet

Miscellaneous order sheet

Par order sheet

Product code

Purveyor order list

Order Sheets

Once the purchasing agent has completed the forecasts and adjustments, he or she must order the food. Like most other management tasks, buying can be facilitated by the appropriate business forms. Although ordering forms appear in a thousand different designs and formats, this book will present three that will handle nearly any purchasing situation.

The first order sheet provides a format for ordering most of the foods a business will need. It is designed to facilitate ordering the same items order after order. The second provides an opportunity for the purchasing agent to receive bids on the business offered, before deciding where to purchase the supplies. The third is a form that lends itself to purchasing miscellaneous items.

Once the purchasing agent has ordered the food, it is helpful to fellow workers if a clear record is left of what was ordered and when it is to arrive. This way, if a question arises regarding when a certain item will arrive, the supervisor should be able to look in the completed order book and find the answer.

The Par Order Sheet

Probably the most common type of order form in use today is one that facilitates par purchasing. Many common types of food are ordered by a low-level par. Specific forecasts are usually calculated for expensive items like meat and seafood, but commonly purchased foods are usually just kept on hand in sufficient quantity. There is an example of a **par order sheet** on page 111.

This form lends itself best to purchasing the same items over and over again. For instance, in a business, a dairy order will probably include items such as milk, cottage cheese, creamers, and sliced American cheese every time. All of these foods are probably purchased with a low-level par. If there are special needs for a particular order time, they can be added to the par forecast. For example, if the low-level par of some market form is 6, and 3 extra will be needed for a special party, add 3 to the par of 6 and forecast 9. Note the following things about this form:

1. "Food Category" refers to the inventory group that is being ordered from this particular form, such as dairy, produce, or baked goods. This sheet is usually limited to orders given to one purveyor, so it contains items from one food category. Although foods of different food categories may be purchased from the same purveyor, this is done infrequently.

2. Since this form provides for ordering the same foods from the same purveyor, it is necessary to write down the purveyor's name and telephone number.

3. The "Item and Description" part of the form contains space to list the foods that are usually ordered from this particular supplier.

4. It may also be worthwhile to list the item's low-level par. The person who normally buys the food may not need this information written down, but it can be handy for someone else who needs to call in an order.

5. Not everyone agrees about what date should be written in the date section. Some write down the date the food was ordered, while others write down the date it is to arrive. The only date that matters to the business is the date the food will arrive in the foodservice so that the production staff can start using it. Record delivery dates only in the date section.

6. Going down the first column, there is space on each line of the order sheet to include the **product code** (PC) of the item. A product code is an identification number, assigned by the supplier, to specifically identify each market form that it sells. By reciting the product code, the purveyor will know exactly what market form is being referred to. Any other description of the product in question can also be listed in this space. When ordering an item, first give the purveyor's order taker the product code, instead of naming the product. Then, he or she can immediately type in the product code and name the product the code was referring to. He or she can also see if the computer is showing sufficient supply of the item to deliver it as requested. He or she may say, "We're just about out of the six-sieve, #10, cut green beans that you want. Can we substitute five sieve?" By identifying possible supply problems at the time of order, substitutions can be approved before they are delivered. Suppliers will provide a catalogue of their product codes for reference.

Par Order Sheet

Food Category:	Purveyor:			Telephone Number: - -			

Item & Description	Low-level Par	Delivery Dates					
PC: _____							
PC: _____							
PC: _____							
PC: _____							
PC: _____							
PC: _____							
PC: _____							
PC: _____							
PC: _____							
PC: _____							
PC: _____							
PC: _____							
PC: _____							
PC: _____							
PC: _____							
PC: _____							
PC: _____							
PC: _____							
PC: _____							
PC: _____							
PC: _____							
PC: _____							
PC: _____							
PC: _____							
PC: _____							
PC: _____							
PC: _____							
PC: _____							
PC: _____							
PC: _____							

7. Use the remainder of the form to write down completed forecasts and orders. Write partially adjusted forecasts in the top half of the square. Then take the order book into the storeroom or cooler and, while looking at the product's inventory (it really isn't necessary to record the inventory), adjust the completed forecast to become an actual order, and record that in the bottom half of the forecast/order square.

The most common way of using this form is to cut it in half along the right edge of the "Low-level Par" column. This leaves the item and description information separate from the ordering part of the form. With the product code and the item's description on the left half of the form, a new order sheet can easily be slipped in when the last one is filled up with orders. This way, the item descriptions won't have to be copied all over again. If a product is needed for a special occasion, it can be added to this form and then ignored until it is needed again.

Again, as a reminder, a par order sheet is often used to purchase baked goods, dairy products, post-mix soda, produce, and ice cream.

A par order sheet, filled out and ready for call-in, is shown on page 113. Study it and see how useful it can be.

Computerizing the Par Order Sheet

Even though many things in a foodservice are purchased with a par order sheet, it is not recommended that the sheet be computerized. Because the par forecast must be adjusted for the current inventory, and because it is so convenient to take the par order sheet into the cooler or storeroom before finalizing an order, the order form will be more useful in a notebook than in a computer. Product codes and other purchasing specifications need to be recorded somewhere, but they can be stored in a purchasing notebook just as well as in a computer.

The Bid Order Sheet

The par order sheet is ideal for ordering the same items from the same purveyor time after time, but for expensive items it's a good idea to inquire about cost before calling in an order. This is where the **bid order sheet** is useful. Page 114 is an example of this form.

Many of the characteristics of this order sheet are like those of the par order sheet. Delivery date, purveyor information, and the item and description space are all the same. But some of the other features are different:

1. The column headed "Order" is designed to contain the final, adjusted order, not just a product's forecast. This is the order amount for call-in.
2. The "Bid" square contains each purveyor's bid price for the commodity. The purchasing agent must be careful to ensure that the bid price is in the same units as the order.
3. The "Cost" square is the extension of that bid price (i.e., the order times that purveyor's bid price).
4. When all bids have been obtained and their respective costs calculated, an invoice total is determined for each bidding supplier.

This order sheet is especially useful as a method of wisely buying expensive items like meat and seafood. It is usually used in two different ways:

1. If the order is large enough, it is split up among suppliers. When the order is large, it may be well worth each supplier's effort to receive only a

Par Order Sheet

113

Food Category: Dairy	Purveyor: The Butter 'N Egg Co.				Telephone Number: 346-174-9020		

Item & Description	Low-level Par	Delivery Dates					
		2/15	2/17	2/19			
PC: 13582		5	5	5			
Milk, whole, 6-gal dispenser	5 each	3 ✔	5 ✔	4 ✔			
PC: 13576		66	66	66			
Milk, skim, 10 oz	66 each	24 ✔	48 ✔	66 ✔			
PC: 13563		144	136	136			
Milk, choc., 10 oz	136 each	144 ✔	110 ✔	136 ✔			
PC: 13542		1	1	1			
Milk, butter, 10 oz	1 each	0	0	0			
PC: 13921		1/2	1/2	2			
Cheese, ched., 10 lb/blk	1/2 blk	1 ✔	0	1 ✔			
PC: 13933		5	5	5			
Cheese, sliced, Am., 3-lb stack	5 stacks	2 ✔	5 ✔	3 ✔			
PC: 13979		1/2	1/2	1/2			
Cheese, Swiss, 10-lb loaf	1/2 loaf	0	1 ✔	0			
PC: 13961		1/2	1/2	1/2			
Cheese, cream, 3-lb loaf	1/2 loaf	0	1 ✔	0			
PC: 13987		1/2	1/2	1/2			
Cheese, parm., 5-lb pail	1/2 pail	1 ✔	1 ✔	1 ✔			
PC: 13995		1	1	1			
Cheese, brie, 2-kg wheel	1 wheel	0	1 ✔	1 ✔			
PC: 13906		1/4	1/4	1/4			
Cheese, prov., 8-lb loaf	1/4 loaf	0	0	1 ✔			
PC: 13981		2	1/4	1/4			
Cheese, mozz., 5-lb loaf	1/4 loaf	2 ✔	0	1 ✔			
PC: 13540		1/2	1/2	1/2			
Sour cream, 5-lb pail	1/2 pail	0	1 ✔	1 ✔			
PC: 13504		3	3	4			
Half & half, ind., 200/cs.	3 cs.	3 ✔	3 ✔	2 ✔			
PC: 13711		2	2	2			
Eggs, large, AA, 30 dz/cs.	2 cs.	1 ✔	2 ✔	2 ✔			
PC: 13649		1	1	1			
Butter, 90 count, 10 lb, 93 score	1 cs.	1 ✔	1 ✔	1 ✔			
PC: 13652		2	2	2			
Margarine, bulk, 30 lb/cs.	2 cs.	1 ✔	1 ✔	2 ✔			
PC: 13974		2					
Cheese, munst., 5-lb loaf	none	2 ✔					
PC: 13913				1			
Cheese, Edam, 12 3 oz/cs.	none			1 ✔			
PC: 13516							
Cream, whipping, qt	none	*Ry*	*Ry*				
PC: 13957							
Cheese, havarti, 5-lb blk	none						
PC: 13583				10			
Milk, whole, gal	none			10 ✔			
PC: _____							
PC: _____			*Ry*				
PC: _____							
PC: _____							

Bid Order Sheet

Delivery Date: / /		Purveyor #1		Purveyor #2		Purveyor #3	
Item & Description	Order	Bid	Cost	Bid	Cost	Bid	Cost
Individual Invoice Total:							

third of the order. Bids are assembled, but in most cases the costs are not calculated nor the totals added; each purveyor is simply awarded that portion of the order for which the lowest price was bid. Low price alone, however, without quality specifications, means little. It is vital to this method of bid ordering that the purchasing agent communicate the product specifications in writing to the bidding suppliers so that they all bid on the same description of the product. This is not difficult if each supplier is given a copy of the foodservice's written specifications when they first start doing business together.

If a buyer is using this method of purchasing, however, he or she should not take advantage of the suppliers. It is expensive to deliver food, so don't make them deliver a single box of bacon, for example, if that is the only low bid. Rather, give the business to one of the other purveyors and pay a little more for that single case.

2. If the order is not large enough to split up and allow each delivering supplier to make some money, don't break it up. Calculate the costs, add up each estimate of the order's total cost from each supplier, and give the entire order to one supplier.

A completed bid order sheet is shown on page 116. There are two options for placing this order. One is to give the entire order to Top Cut Meats, the supplier who will charge the least for the whole order. The other is to split up the order and give each item to the lowest bidder, as circled on the sheet. This will also give Top Cut Meats the biggest part of the order, but the order is big enough so that all three purveyors should be able to make some money.

Computerizing the Bid Order Sheet

If the order is to be split up among the bidders, there is really no need to computerize this form. None of the information it contains needs to be saved for record, and it requires no calculations. However, the computer is as handy a place to do such work as a handwritten notebook, so an example of how this order sheet is to be set up is provided on page 117. In this example, the losing bids have been erased to avoid misreading at call-in time.

Spreadsheet programs are made to assist calculations, so this form is best put to a spreadsheet if the order is not to be split up and depends on the lowest invoice. Here the computer can automatically extend each bid price so each total invoice can be determined. See the example of this on page 118. The formulas in the extension part of this worksheet are straightforward. For example, the formula contained in cell G4 is B4*D4.

The only thing that may create confusion is the placement of the invoice totals on the sheet itself. These totals were placed in columns D, E, and F because of the width of most viewscreens. To see the entire spreadsheet, the program would have to be shifted right. This is unnecessary, since extensions do not need to be seen, just the invoice totals. These totals make use of another of the functions found in most spreadsheet programs, the SUM function. This function adds the values in a range. The formula in cell D29 is @ SUM (G4..G27). If the spreadsheet is set up in this manner, both options of this form can be used, depending on the day's ordering needs.

The Miscellaneous Order Sheet

The **miscellaneous order sheet** allows the buyer to purchase those items that are needed only once in a while and therefore have no need of a par. This is the form usually used to buy groceries. Particularly with a cycle menu, many

Bid Order Sheet

Item & Description	Order	Purveyor #1 Dixie Meat		Purveyor #2 Top Cut Meat		Purveyor #3 Al's Meat Co.	
Delivery Date: 7/27/06		Bid	Cost	Bid	Cost	Bid	Cost
Hamburger, bulk, 80/20	30 lb ✔	1.79	53.70	(1.68)	50.40	1.83	54.90
Hamburger, pats, 4/1	20 lb ✔	1.81	36.20	(1.70)	34.00	1.85	37.00
Hamburger, pats, 8/1	60 lb ✔	1.81	108.60	(1.70)	102.00	1.85	111.00
Inside round, choi, 20 lb	73 lb ✔	2.48	181.04	(2.35)	171.55	2.63	191.99
Tenderloin, choi, PSMO	18 lb ✔	5.38	96.84	(5.27)	94.86	5.41	97.38
NY strip, choi, 12 oz ea.	35 ea. ✔	4.16	145.60	(4.13)	144.55	4.36	152.60
Pork loin, BRT	27 lb ✔	3.64	98.28	3.62	97.74	(3.59)	96.93
Pork chop, CC, 3/1	10 lb ✔	3.15	31.50	3.12	31.20	(3.08)	30.80
Pork stew, 1/2" cube	20 lb ✔	(1.86)	37.20	1.89	37.80	1.89	37.80
Bacon, hotel, 18-22	30 lb ✔	2.15	64.50	(2.14)	64.20	2.17	65.10
Ham, 4x4 Pullman, picnic	22 lb ✔	2.46	54.12	2.46	54.12	(2.41)	53.02
Hot dogs, AB, 8/1	20 lb ✔	(1.92)	38.40	1.97	39.40	1.95	39.00
Hot dogs, AB, 4/1	40 lb ✔	(1.92)	76.80	1.97	78.80	1.95	78.00
Kielbasa	8 lb ✔	2.00	16.00	(1.98)	15.84	1.99	15.92
Turkey brst, ckd, bnls	12 lb ✔	(2.84)	34.08	2.86	34.32	2.93	35.16
Chix, 1/4s, 2-1/2 lb, A	35 hd ✔	2.03	71.05	(2.00)	70.00	2.01	70.35
Salami, Genoa	10 lb ✔	5.16	51.60	5.21	52.10	(4.99)	49.90
Bologna	10 lb ✔	1.89	18.90	(1.86)	18.60	1.87	18.70
Chix brst, 48 S/cs., 5 oz	3 cs. ✔	(34.88)	104.64	34.99	104.97	35.16	105.48
		Ry					
Individual Invoice Total:			1319.05		(1296.45)		1341.03

	A	B	C	D	E	F
1	**Bid Order Sheet**					
2					Bid	
3	Item	Order	Order Unit	Dixie	Tru Value	Mike's
4	Inside	35	lb	$2.36		
5	Outside	0	lb			
6	Hamburger	60	lb			$1.51
7	Beef pat	3	10 lb			$15.13
8	109 rib	0	lb			
9	Top butt	0	lb			
10	12 oz strip	15	each		$4.71	
11	8 oz filet	7	each		$3.11	
12	18 oz Porter	11	each			$5.92
13	5 oz cubed	0	lb			
14	Ckd C B	6	lb	$1.99		
15	Pork loin	0	lb			
16	4x4 Pullman	2	11 lb	$19.36		
17	Ham bnls	0	lb			
18	5 oz P chop	17	lb	$2.51		
19	Bacon	2	12 lb	$24.12		
20	Hot dog	3	10 lb		$18.22	
21	Polish	0	lb			
22	Italian	0	lb			
23	Fryer	75	head			$2.21
24	Turk brst	10	lb			$2.79
25	Chix kiev	0	96/case			
26	Catfish	21	5 lb	$1.83		
27	Shrimp	0	3 lb			
28						
29						

items may only be used a few times each month, so it is not worth establishing either kind of par for them.

There is an example of a miscellaneous order sheet on page 119. There are no elements of this form that have not already been seen on the par order sheet or the bid order sheet. A completed miscellaneous order sheet is on page 120.

Computerizing the Miscellaneous Order Sheet

The miscellaneous order spreadsheet is one of the simplest of those discussed so far. It is a good one for the manager to set up, not for calculations but for record.

The record to be kept on this sheet is product codes. As indicated earlier, the use of product codes is a sound purchasing practice. Every purchasing agent should use them to avoid call-in confusion, but they are time consuming to look up initially. Once they have been looked up for an order, the manager doesn't have time to look them up again for the next order, so they must be recorded somewhere to be handy when needed. In fact, it is a good thing to record at least the supplier's product code and the item designation for each item ordered, even if it's only ordered occasionally. And, like some other data, the spreadsheet is a convenient place to record them.

The spreadsheets on pages 121, 122, and 123 are examples of one way this material could be organized. In this case the worksheet contains a list of all of the groceries purchased from the grocery purveyor, even if they are

Bid Order Sheet

	A	B	C	D	E	F	G	H	I
1	**Bid Order Sheet**								
2					Bid			Extension	
3	Item	Order	Order Unit	Dixie	Tru Value	Mike's	Dixie	Tru Value	Mike's
4	Inside	35	lb	$2.36	$2.63	$2.51	$82.60	$92.05	$87.85
5	Outside	0	lb	$0.00	$0.00	$0.00	$0.00	$0.00	$0.00
6	Hamburger	60	lb	$1.67	$1.86	$1.51	$100.20	$111.60	$90.60
7	Beef pat	3	10 lb	$16.72	$18.66	$15.13	$50.16	$55.98	$45.39
8	109 rib	0	lb	$0.00	$0.00	$0.00	$0.00	$0.00	$0.00
9	Top butt	0	lb	$0.00	$0.00	$0.00	$0.00	$0.00	$0.00
10	12 oz strip	15	each	$4.86	$4.71	$5.01	$72.90	$70.65	$75.15
11	8 oz filet	7	each	$3.25	$3.11	$3.25	$22.75	$21.77	$22.75
12	18 oz Porter	11	each	$6.17	$5.99	$5.92	$67.87	$65.89	$65.12
13	5 oz cubed	0	lb	$0.00	$0.00	$0.00	$0.00	$0.00	$0.00
14	Ckd C B	6	lb	$1.99	$2.03	$2.01	$11.94	$12.18	$12.06
15	Pork loin	0	lb	$0.00	$0.00	$0.00	$0.00	$0.00	$0.00
16	4x4 Pullman	2	11 lb	$19.36	$19.75	$19.52	$38.72	$39.50	$39.04
17	Ham bnls	0	lb	$0.00	$0.00	$0.00	$0.00	$0.00	$0.00
18	5 oz P chop	17	lb	$2.51	$2.68	$2.66	$42.67	$45.56	$45.22
19	Bacon	2	12 lb	$24.12	$24.37	$25.11	$48.24	$48.74	$50.22
20	Hot dog	3	10 lb	$18.60	$18.22	$18.34	$55.80	$54.66	$55.02
21	Polish	0	lb	$0.00	$0.00	$0.00	$0.00	$0.00	$0.00
22	Italian	0	lb	$0.00	$0.00	$0.00	$0.00	$0.00	$0.00
23	Fryer	75	head	$2.37	$2.41	$2.21	$177.75	$180.75	$165.75
24	Turk brst	10	lb	$2.85	$2.81	$2.79	$28.50	$28.10	$27.90
25	Chix kiev	0	96/case	$0.00	$0.00	$0.00	$0.00	$0.00	$0.00
26	Catfish	21	5 lb	$1.83	$1.96	$1.91	$38.43	$41.16	$40.11
27	Shrimp	0	3 lb	$0.00	$0.00	$0.00	$0.00	$0.00	$0.00
28									
29			Invoice Total	$838.53	$868.59	$822.18			

Miscellaneous Order Sheet

| Delivery Date: / / | Purveyor: | | Telephone Number: - - |

Product Code	Order	Item & Description

Miscellaneous Order Sheet

Delivery Date:	12/6/92	Purveyor: Morrison Supply Company		Telephone Number: 326-499-0607

Product Code	Order	Item & Description
G-10765	2 cs. ✔	Corn, cut, 6 #10/cs. all canned goods blue label quality
G-25411	3 cs. ✔	Green beans, cut, blue lake, #5 sieve, 6 #10/cs.
G-46829	1 cs. ✔	Peach halves, heavy syrup, 40-45 count, 6 #10/cs.
G-62221	1 cs. ✔	Peach slices, heavy syrup, 6 #10/cs.
G-92576	3 cs. ✔	Pear halves, light syrup, 40-45 count, 6 #10/cs.
G-37213	5 cs. ✔	Tomatoes, pieces, in juice, 6 #10/cs.
G-37274	2 cs. ✔	Tomatoes, puree, 6 #10/cs.
G-37286	3 cs. ✔	Tomatoes, paste, specific gravity 1.07, 6 #10/cs.
B-74002	5 cs. ✔	Coffee, 12-oz bags, 48 bags/cs.
B-38794	1 cs. ✔	Nedlog fruit drink syrup, grape, mix 4:1, 4 gal/cs.
B-38795	2 cs. ✔	Nedlog fruit drink syrup, orange, mix 4:1, 4 gal/cs.
B-65312	1 cs. ✔	Tea bags, orange pekoe, English breakfast, 10 100/cs.
F-98133	4 cs. ✔	French fries, shoestring, 27 lb/cs.
F-16793	2 cs. ✔	Peas, early june, 12 3 lb/cs.
F-76118	3 cs. ✔	Winter mix, broc-caul-carr, 12 2.5 lb/cs.
F-11172	1 cs. ✔	Onion rings, 12 2.5 lb/cs.
F-23783	2 cs. ✔	Broccoli, whole, 12 2 lb/cs.
F-22551	3 cs. ✔	Mixed vegetables, 12 3 lb/cs.
D-19283	1 cs. ✔	Vermicelli, 20 lb/cs.
D-16331	2 sacks ✔	Flour, bread, CWT/sack
D-36784	3 sacks ✔	Sugar, fine, 25 lb/sack
D-36788	4 cs. ✔	Sugar packets, 2,000/cs.
D-19254	1 cs. ✔	Egg noodles, broad, 10 lb/cs.
D-41795	1 cs. ✔	Corn starch, 12 1 lb/cs.
S-49536	1 can ✔	Garlic powder, 1 lb/can
S-96552	1 can ✔	Basil, ground, 1 lb/can
	Ry	

	A	B	C	D	E
1					
2	**Miscellaneous Order Sheet**				
3					
4	Prod Code	Item	Pack	Order	Indicator
5	13827	Pear 1/2	6 #10	1	0
6	13902	Peach 1/2	6 #10	3	1
7	13904	Peach sl	6 #10	2	0
8	14052	Pine ring	6 #10	1	0
9	14054	Pine chunk	6 #10	1	1
10	14066	F cocktail	6 #10	4	1
11	14378	M cherry	4 1/2 gal	1	0
12	14631	Apple sc	6 #10	1	0
13	14718	C apple	6 #10	1	0
14	15001	Corn	6 #10	2	1
15	15027	G bns cut	6 #10	3	1
16	15029	G bns FC	6 #10	1	1
17	15033	G bns Wh	6 #10	3	0
18	15034	W bns cut	6 #10	2	0
19	16002	1000 Isl	4 gal	1	0
20	16004	Bleu cheese	4 gal	2	1
21	16009	Ranch	4 gal	1	1
22	16014	Russian	4 gal	2	0
23	16019	French	4 gal	1	1
24	16026	Italian	4 gal	2	1
25	16034	Mayo	4 gal	3	1
26	16057	Vinegar	12 qt	1	0
27	16063	Salad oil	5 gal	2	1
28	16066	Frymax	6 2.5 qt	3	1
29	16067	Sweetex	50 lb	1	0
30	16068	Primex	50 lb	1	1
31	17023	Corn strch	24 1 lb	1	0
32	17027	AP flour	CWT	2	1
33	17028	Bred flour	CWT	1	0
34	17031	Past flour	CWT	2	0
35	17226	Rice	25 lb	2	0
36	17328	Sugar gran	25 lb	2	1
37	17330	Sugar pwd	24 1 lb	1	0
38	17336	Sugar brn	12 2 lb	1	0
39	17341	Salt	24 1 lb	1	1
40	18540	Catsup	6 #10	2	1
41	18552	Mustard	4 gal	1	1
42	18556	H Radish	12 qt	1	0
43	18631	D Pickle	5 gal	1	1
44	18657	P Relish	4 gal	1	0
45	18711	Sport pep	4 gal	1	0
46	19223	Garlic pwd	1 lb	1	1
47	19224	Garlic slt	1 lb	1	0
48	19312	Oregano	5 lb	1	0
49	19356	B Pepper	1 lb	1	1
50	19357	W Pepper	1 lb	1	0
51	19402	Basil	1 lb	1	0
52	21017	Coffee	72 3 oz	4	1
53	21211	Tea	10 100	1	1
54	21359	Hot choco	4 50	1	1
55	21637	F Punch	4 gal	2	0
56					
57					
58					
59					

	A	B	C	D	E
1					
2	**Miscellaneous Order Sheet**				
3					
4	Prod Code	Item	Pack	Order	Indicator
5	13902	Peach 1/2	6 #10	3	1
6	21017	Coffee	72 3 oz	4	1
7	18631	D Pickle	5 gal	1	1
8	18540	Catsup	6 #10	2	1
9	16066	Frymax	6 2.5 qt	3	1
10	14054	Pine chunk	6 #10	1	1
11	14066	F cocktail	6 #10	4	1
12	17328	Sugar gran	25 lb	2	1
13	18552	Mustard	4 gal	1	1
14	15027	G bns cut	6 #10	3	1
15	16063	Salad oil	5 gal	2	1
16	16019	French	4 gal	1	1
17	16026	Italian	4 gal	2	1
18	16068	Primex	50 lb	1	1
19	16034	Mayo	4 gal	3	1
20	17341	Salt	24 1 lb	1	1
21	19356	B Pepper	1 lb	1	1
22	19223	Garlic pwd	1 lb	1	1
23	16004	Bleu cheese	4 gal	2	1
24	21359	Hot choco	4 50	1	1
25	15029	G bns FC	6 #10	1	1
26	21211	Tea	10 100	1	1
27	15001	Corn	6 #10	2	1
28	16009	Ranch	4 gal	1	1
29	17027	AP flour	CWT	2	1
30	18556	H Radish	12 qt	1	0
31	17336	Sugar brn	12 2 lb	1	0
32	19312	Oregano	5 lb	1	0
33	14052	Pine ring	6 #10	1	0
34	13827	Pear 1/2	6 #10	1	0
35	18657	P Relish	4 gal	1	0
36	17028	Bred flour	CWT	1	0
37	19402	Basil	1 lb	1	0
38	21637	F Punch	4 gal	2	0
39	14718	C Apple	6 #10	1	0
40	18711	Sport pep	4 gal	1	0
41	17023	Corn strch	24 1 lb	1	0
42	14631	Apple Sc	6 #10	1	0
43	16002	1000 Isl	4 gal	1	0
44	17031	Past flour	CWT	2	0
45	16067	Sweetex	50 lb	1	0
46	16014	Russian	4 gal	2	0
47	13904	Peach sl	6 #10	2	0
48	15034	W Bns cut	6 #10	2	0
49	19224	Garlic slt	1 lb	1	0
50	15033	G Bns Wh	6 #10	3	0
51	16057	Vinegar	12 qt	1	0
52	17226	Rice	25 lb	2	0
53	19357	W Pepper	1 lb	1	0
54	14378	M Cherry	4 1/2 gal	1	0
55	17330	Sugar pwd	24 1 lb	1	0
56					
57					
58					
59					

	A	B	C	D	E
1					
2	**Miscellaneous Order Sheet**				
3					
4	Prod Code	Item	Pack	Order	Indicator
5	13827	Pear 1/2	6 #10	1	0
6	13902	Peach 1/2	6 #10	3	0
7	13904	Peach sl	6 #10	2	0
8	14052	Pine ring	6 #10	1	0
9	14054	Pine chunk	6 #10	1	0
10	14066	F cocktail	6 #10	4	0
11	14378	M cherry	4 1/2 gal	1	0
12	14631	Apple Sc	6 #10	1	0
13	14718	C apple	6 #10	1	0
14	15001	Corn	6 #10	2	0
15	15027	G bns cut	6 #10	3	0
16	15029	G bns FC	6 #10	1	0
17	15033	G bns Wh	6 #10	3	0
18	15034	W Bns cut	6 #10	2	0
19	16002	1000 Isl	4 gal	1	0
20	16004	Bleu cheese	4 gal	2	0
21	16009	Ranch	4 gal	1	0
22	16014	Russian	4 gal	2	0
23	16019	French	4 gal	1	0
24	16026	Italian	4 gal	2	0
25	16034	Mayo	4 gal	3	0
26	16057	Vinegar	12 qt	1	0
27	16063	Salad oil	5 gal	2	0
28	16066	Frymax	6 2.5 qt	3	0
29	16067	Sweetex	50 lb	1	0
30	16068	Primex	50 lb	1	0
31	17023	Corn strch	24 1 lb	1	0
32	17027	AP flour	CWT	2	0
33	17028	Bred flour	CWT	1	0
34	17031	Past flour	CWT	2	0
35	17226	Rice	25 lb	2	0
36	17328	Sugar gran	25 lb	2	0
37	17330	Sugar pwd	24 1 lb	1	0
38	17336	Sugar brn	12 2 lb	1	0
39	17341	Salt	24 1 lb	1	0
40	18540	Catsup	6 #10	2	0
41	18552	Mustard	4 gal	1	0
42	18556	H Radish	12 qt	1	0
43	18631	D Pickle	5 gal	1	0
44	18657	P Relish	4 gal	1	0
45	18711	Sport pep	4 gal	1	0
46	19223	Garlic pwd	1 lb	1	0
47	19224	Garlic slt	1 lb	1	0
48	19312	Oregano	5 lb	1	0
49	19356	B Pepper	1 lb	1	0
50	19357	W Pepper	1 lb	1	0
51	19402	Basil	1 lb	1	0
52	21017	Coffee	72 3 oz	4	0
53	21211	Tea	10 100	1	0
54	21359	Hot choco	4 50	1	0
55	21637	F Punch	4 gal	2	0
56					
57					
58					
59					

purchased only occasionally. As new items are added to the list from time to time, their respective product codes are also recorded so that the list is a complete order list at all times. The "Pack" column, column C, lists the number of units per case. The "Order" column, column D, is where potential orders are recorded. Only column E, the "Indicator" column, may require some explanation.

Column E is an indicator of which order numbers are for the current order, and which order numbers are old and to be ignored. As each new order is received (order data should not be discarded until the food is actually received), the number in the order column could be changed to zero, but as we shall see with the use of the indicator column, this is unnecessary. The spreadsheet on page 121 shows how the sheet will look after the purchasing agent has keyed in the order. To do this, the buyer scrolls down the list of the items until he or she runs across an item wanted on this order. When one of these items is reached, the number of cases is typed in and then the zero in the indicator column is changed to a one, indicating that this item is to be ordered currently. When this process is completed, a sheet like the one on page 121 results and contains the new orders, and a series of ones and zeros in the indicator column.

Just before call-in time, the buyer should have the program sort the list so all of the items to be ordered this time are together. All spreadsheet programs have a SORT function that allows the program to sort the data on the sheet, by any row or column, in ascending or descending order. So, the buyer sorts the list by column E, the indicator column, in descending order, and all of the items desired on the new order are together at the top of the list (see page 122). Now the buyer is ready to call in the order.

When talking to the purveyor, the buyer keeps the computer's cursor in the indicator column and orders the food. That is, the product code is given to the purveyor, who types it into the computer and confirms what the buyer wants by naming the product in question. Then the buyer orders the number of cases wanted, and changes the one in the indicator column to a zero, indicating that the item is ordered. Then he or she moves on to the next item, and so on down the list, until everything has been ordered. When the buyer has ordered everything, all of the numbers in the indicator column are zero, and the list is ready for the next order.

When it is time to prepare for the next order, the buyer should sort the list again, only this time by the product code column, column A, in ascending order. This returns the food list to its original form, as seen on page 123. And the buyer can then key in the new order as was done on page 121).

Calling in the Order

Once one or more of these forms have been used to organize the order, the supplier must be called. The beginner might appreciate a few hints. While ordering, check off each amount while actually ordering it. Checking items off helps to keep one's place on the list. After the order is done, it's a good idea to add one's initials at the end of the list. This tells anyone interested who called in the order, that it was completed, and that it can be expected to arrive on the date given on the order sheet.

The Purveyor Order List

It is also very helpful to include all of the pertinent purchasing information needed on a form called the **purveyor order list** in the front of the order book. Information such as where each type of commodity is purchased, what the usual delivery days are, what the purveyors' telephone numbers are, and so forth, will help the substitute buyer.

Dailies

It is also helpful to have a permanent notebook that only has six or seven pages in it, one for each day of the week that the business is open. Assign one page for each day of the week, and then list on it all the things that should be done that day. On Friday, for instance, one might list:

1. Order bread for Monday delivery.
2. Order dairy for Monday delivery.
3. Order produce for Monday delivery.
4. Turn in payroll.
5. Fill out income statement.

This can be a great help on a busy day, and it is invaluable to a substitute.

Appendix: Measure Conversion

In business, quantities often need to be converted from the form in which they are presented. For example, if two gallons of milk are needed but milk is supplied only in a quart measure, a conversion will be necessary. Frequently, as well, conversion to another expression or label will simply be more convenient. Conversion is not difficult, but does require practice.

KEY TERM

Unit of conversion

Conversion

When working in the foodservice business, it is often necessary to change the form of a measurement. For example, if a baking formula calls for a teaspoon of vanilla and one is asked to increase the formula 1,000 times, it is not realistic to measure one teaspoon 1,000 times. The measurement needs to be converted to a more manageable quantity (e.g., gallons rather than teaspoons). The change from teaspoons to gallons does not make more or less vanilla, but only makes the measurement more manageable.

The following is a review of some basic mathematical concepts:

1. The value of anything divided by itself is one:

$$\frac{1}{1} = 1 \qquad \frac{A}{A} = 1$$

2. Anything can be multiplied by 1 without changing its value:

$$3 \times 1 = 3 \qquad L \times 1 = L \qquad AB \times 1 = AB$$

3. Labels can be multiplied, divided, and canceled in exactly the same way as numbers:

$$2 \times 2 = 2^2 \qquad A \times B = AB \qquad \frac{AB}{B} = A$$

$$3 \text{ ft.} \times 4 \text{ ft.} \times 6 \text{ ft.} = 72 \text{ ft.}^3$$

(Note that the label in the last example is now "cubic feet" and was determined by multiplying, the same process used in calculating the 72.)

That done, let's combine these concepts with the idea that conversion does not change amounts or sizes. The last tool one needs to convert is a mathematical pattern referred to in this workbook as a **unit of conversion**, or UOC. Here is an example of a unit of conversion:

$$\frac{36 \text{ in.}}{1 \text{ yd.}}$$

A UOC has three characteristics:

1. It has a value of 1. Since 36 inches is the same as 1 yard, the value of this expression is one (anything divided by itself is one).

2. It is the key to conversion between the labels shown. Any situation requiring the conversion of inches to yards, or yards to inches, can be completed using this UOC.

3. Its value does not change if it is written upside down:

$$\frac{36 \text{ in.}}{1 \text{ yd.}} = \frac{1 \text{ yd.}}{36 \text{ in.}}$$

There are an endless number of UOCs—at least one for every conversion problem possible. Here are some examples:

$$\frac{5{,}280 \text{ ft.}}{1 \text{ mi.}} \qquad \frac{0.947 \text{ L}}{1 \text{ qt}} \qquad \frac{16 \text{ Tbsp}}{1 \text{ cup}} \qquad \frac{60 \text{ min.}}{1 \text{ hr.}} \qquad \frac{3 \text{ ft.}}{1 \text{ yd.}}$$

The best technique for converting one measurement to another is to manipulate their labels until the only label left is the one needed in the answer. Here is a simple example:

EXAMPLE

How many hours are there in 727 minutes?

Solution

You can divide 727 by 60 and successfully convert the amount of time in minutes to an equal amount of time measured in hours:

$$\frac{727}{60} = 12.117$$

That was easy, but some conversions get complicated and occasionally it is difficult to decide whether to multiply or divide. Here is the same conversion problem illustrating conversion by manipulating labels using a UOC:

$$727 \text{ min.} \times \frac{1 \text{ hr.}}{60 \text{ min.}} = ?$$

In this example, the quantity we are converting has been multiplied by the appropriate UOC. Before we divide by 60, let's make a few observations:

1. In the above statement of the problem, 727 minutes could be written as

$$\frac{727 \text{ min.}}{1}$$

This illustrates that "727 min." can be considered the numerator of a fraction.

2. Notice that, in this approach to the solution, 727 minutes is multiplied by the UOC

$$\frac{1 \text{ hr.}}{60 \text{ min.}}$$

This doesn't change the value of 727 minutes, since anything multiplied by 1 is itself.

If we turn away from the numbers, watch what happens to the labels:

$$727 \text{ min.} \times \frac{1 \text{ hr.}}{60 \text{ min.}} = ? \text{ hrs.}$$

The minutes cancel and the remaining arithmetic expression is labeled hours. Whatever number results, the quantity will be in hours. Solving the remaining arithmetic expression will complete the problem:

$$727 \text{ min.} \times \frac{1 \text{ hr.}}{60 \text{ min.}} = \frac{727 \text{ hr.}}{60} = 12.117 \text{ hr.}$$

The above process is often startling to people just beginning to convert, but if the labels are manipulated properly the numbers will automatically build an arithmetic expression that will solve the problem.

EXAMPLE

How many miles are in 12,000,000 inches?

Solution

Since the number of inches in a mile is not commonly known, we don't have a UOC that will complete the problem in one step. It will probably take two UOCs to do the job. Using

$$\frac{1 \text{ ft.}}{12 \text{ in.}} \quad \text{and} \quad \frac{1 \text{ mi.}}{5,280 \text{ ft.}}$$

we should be able to complete the work. Here's how it's done:

$$12,000,000 \text{ in.} \times \frac{1 \text{ ft.}}{12 \text{ in.}} \times \frac{1 \text{ mi.}}{5,280 \text{ ft.}} = ? \text{ mi.}$$

The first UOC is used to convert inches to feet and the second to convert feet to miles. Once the labels have been canceled, the numbers can be consolidated and the problem solved.

1. First consolidate the numerator. The only number in the numerator is 12,000,000.

2. Now consolidate the denominator. That is $12 \times 5,280$.

3. The resulting fraction is

$$\frac{12,000,000}{12 \times 5,280}$$

(Since the only label left is miles, these numbers represent miles.)

The whole problem flows like this:

$$12{,}000{,}000 \text{ in.} \times \frac{1 \text{ ft.}}{12 \text{ in.}} \times \frac{1 \text{ mi.}}{5{,}280 \text{ ft.}} = \frac{12{,}000{,}000 \text{ mi.}}{12 \times 5{,}280} = \frac{12{,}000{,}000 \text{ mi.}}{63{,}360}$$

$$= 189.394 \text{ mi.}$$

Notice that the problem almost solved itself as labels were canceled to reach the desired label, miles. It was not necessary to decide whether to multiply or divide these numbers.

Be careful when writing a UOC to keep numbers with their proper labels. For example,

$$\frac{36 \text{ in.}}{1 \text{ yd.}}$$

can be written as its inverse,

$$\frac{1 \text{ yd.}}{36 \text{ in.}}$$

but the numbers can never be switched from their respective labels:

$$\frac{36 \text{ yd.}}{1 \text{ in.}}$$

is never correct.

Here is a step-by-step procedure for conversion:

1. Identify the label on the initial quantity.
2. Define the label you want in your answer.
3. Multiply the initial quantity by one or more units of conversion, canceling labels as you go, until the desired label in the answer is reached.
4. Consolidate the numbers and solve the arithmetic portion of the problem.

▮▮▮▮▮ EXAMPLE

How many quarts are there in 540 tsp?

Solution

The difficult part in conversion is knowing which UOC to use next so that each UOC leads you on to the next label needed and finally to the label in the answer. In this case each UOC used should result in a larger label in the numerator:

$$540 \text{ tsp} \times \frac{1 \text{ Tbsp}}{3 \text{ tsp}} \times \frac{1 \text{ cup}}{16 \text{ Tbsp}} \times \frac{1 \text{ qt}}{4 \text{ cup}} = \frac{540 \text{ qt}}{3 \times 16 \times 4} = \frac{540 \text{ qt}}{192} = 2.813 \text{ qt}$$

As you may already see, the above problem can be solved in two ways with a calculator.

1. Multiply out the denominator, make note of it, and then do the final division to solve the expression.
2. You can also do the problem continuously without ever taking it out of

the calculator. Follow along with your calculator to see the example. Clear the machine and press the buttons in the following order:

$$540 \div 3 \div 16 \div 4 =$$

and 2.813 will appear. This is a faster method but may be a little confusing if you don't follow the algebra. Remember that the 3, the 16, and the 4 are all in a divisory position relative to the 540. It does not matter if you divide by the entire denominator all at once, or by the 3, then the 16, and then the 4 individually. If you use this method, you can leave the entire problem in the calculator at all times and won't need to do it in stages.

Don't miss out on the simplicity of placing the UOCs. If the unwanted label is in the numerator of the initial quantity, write the UOC so that its unwanted label appears in the denominator of the UOC to make that particular label cancel. The numbers will automatically fall into their proper places to solve the problem.

The Metric System

The conversion process is important to anyone using a European recipe in the United States. Our system of numbering, which is based on tens, makes sense. However, our system of measurement does not make a great deal of sense: there are 5,280 feet in a mile, 12 inches in a foot, 3 feet in a yard, 4 cups to a quart, and 16 tablespoons to a cup. None of these is based on tens, and conversion becomes difficult. Another shortcoming in the English system of measurement is that the small unit of weight is called an ounce and the small unit of volume is *also* called an ounce; two completely different quantities are identified by the same label.

Here to refresh your memory is a diagram of our numbering system:

millions	100 thousands	10 thousands	thousands	hundreds	tens	ones	tenths	hundredths	thousandths	10-thousandths	100-thousandths	millionths
0,	0	0	0,	0	0	0.	0	0	0,	0	0	0

As you know, each column's value is ten times greater than that of the column to its right. The metric system uses the same base ten idea. It has simply assigned different names to the columns.

kilo	hecto	deka	units	deci	centi	milli
0,	0	0	0.	0	0	0

The names of these columns in the metric system are
The superiority of the metric system surfaces when dealing with measurement conversion. All measurement in the metric system is based on tens. If the unit measurement is grams, a thousand of them will be called a kilogram. A meter is a tenth of a dekameter and is also a one thousandth of a

kilometer. The metric measurements that appear in the units column are, for example, grams, meters, and liters. It would be proper, when talking about 1,500 grams, to describe it as 1.5 kilograms or even 15 hectograms. The conversion from grams to kilograms or to hectograms is simply a matter of multiplying or dividing the original quantity by tens. Conversion within the metric system can therefore be accomplished by simply moving the decimal point, and requires no complicated calculations.

Study the above prefixes to see how metric conversion works. Work out for yourself that 752 cm = 7.52 m, that 0.099 km = 99 m, that 213 L = .213 kL, or that 16 kg = 16,000 gm. This may take a little practice, but study the idea of metric conversion until you can easily hop from grams to kilograms and even back to milligrams if needed.

Here are some important measurement equivalents to memorize.

Weight

16 oz = 1 lb	1,000 gm = 1 kg
2.2 lb = 1 kg	

Volume

3 tsp = 1 Tbsp	16 Tbsp = 1 cup
2 cup = 1 pt	2 pt = 1 qt
4 qt = 1 gal	2 Tbsp = 1 oz
8 oz = 1 cup	32 oz = 1 qt
128 oz = 1 gal	1 cm^3 = 1 ml
1,000 ml = 1 L	0.947 L = 1 qt

Ladle—number on the handle is the capacity of the bowl in ounces.

Scoop—sometimes called a disher. The number on the wire in the bowl signifies how many of that size scoop it takes to make a quart. A #16 scoop is a 2-oz scoop, since it takes 16 to make a quart.

Length

12 in. = 1 ft.	3 ft. = 1 yd.
5,280 ft. = 1 mi.	1,000 m = 1 km
100 cm = 1 m	1,000 mm = 1 m
1 m = 39.37 in.	

Temperature

212° Fahrenheit = boiling point of water

100° Centigrade or Celsius = boiling point of water

32° Fahrenheit = freezing point of water

0° Centigrade = freezing point of water

Weight to Volume

Sixteen ounces of water weigh 1 lb or, as the saying goes, "A pint's a pound the world around." A cubic centimeter of water has a volume of one ml and weighs one gram. Be very careful when going back and forth between weight and volume. A pint of water does weigh 1 lb, and a gram of water does have a volume of 1 ml, but water is the *only* substance for which this is true. In cooking one often makes the assumption that "a pint's a pound" for any liquid, but it's only true for water. It's usually close enough, but always be watchful when you use this simple conversion for other liquids. If you want to find an exact weight to volume conversion for an ingredient, look up the procedure in a high school physics or chemistry book under "specific gravity." In most cases, however, you can use "a pint's a pound."

Here are some more complicated examples of conversion.

EXAMPLE

How many grams are there in 53 oz?

Solution

Remember the rules for conversion.

1. Begin with ounces.
2. Look for grams.
3. Since you're going from the English system to the metric system, at some point you will need to use this UOC:

$$\frac{1 \text{ kg}}{2.2 \text{ lb}}$$

If you have ounces to start with, however, you can't use that particular UOC because it requires pounds to lead into its use. So you'll have to convert the ounces to pounds first. When you have progressed that far, you'll end up with kilograms. That's not what you're looking for in the answer either, so you'll have to further convert those kilograms to grams. It looks like three UOCs will be needed to successfully make this conversion. Watch how the solution builds itself:

$$53 \text{ oz} \times \frac{1 \text{ lb}}{16 \text{ oz}} \text{ will equal pounds.}$$

$$53 \text{ oz} \times \frac{1 \text{ lb}}{16 \text{ oz}} \times \frac{1 \text{ kg}}{2.2 \text{ lb}} \text{ will equal kilograms.}$$

$$53 \text{ oz} \times \frac{1 \text{ lb}}{16 \text{ oz}} \times \frac{1 \text{ kg}}{2.2 \text{ lb}} \times \frac{1,000 \text{ gm}}{1 \text{ kg}} = ? \text{ gm}$$

Now the problem is set up. Notice that when an unwanted label appeared in the numerator, the UOC was written so that the unwanted label was part of the denominator.

4. Consolidate the arithmetic:

$$53 \text{ oz} \times \frac{1 \text{ lb}}{16 \text{ oz}} \times \frac{1 \text{ kg}}{2.2 \text{ lb}} \times \frac{1,000 \text{ gm}}{1 \text{ kg}} = \frac{53 \times 1,000 \text{ gm}}{16 \times 2.2} = 1,505.682 \text{ gm}$$

EXAMPLE

How many inches are there in 85 cm?

Solution

1. Start with centimeters.
2. End up with inches.
3.
$$85 \text{ cm} \times \frac{1 \text{ m}}{100 \text{ cm}} \times \frac{39.37 \text{ in.}}{1 \text{ m}} = ? \text{ in.}$$

4. Consolidating the arithmetic, you get

$$\frac{85 \times 39.37 \text{ in.}}{100} = 33.465 \text{ in.}$$

Conversion is also useful for increasing or decreasing recipes or formulas. For example, ounces can be increased into pounds of ingredients as a recipe expands to fit a particular group size. A recipe from France in metric measurement can even be made useful to an American cook, if one can do the converting. Conversion is also useful when a foodservice planner needs to express the expected consumption of a group in actual cases of food.

▓▓▓▓▓ **EXAMPLE**

How many boxes of 8/1 (eight servings to the pound) hot dogs will you need to feed 725 people two hot dogs each? Hot dogs come in 10-lb boxes.

Solution

The problem is to convert people to boxes of hot dogs, or

$$\frac{725 \text{ people}}{\text{party}} = \frac{? \text{ boxes}}{\text{party}}$$

1. "People at the party" is the label on the initial quantity.
2. "Boxes for the party" should be the label in the answer.
3. $\dfrac{725 \text{ people}}{\text{party}} \times \dfrac{2 \text{ servings}}{\text{person}} \times \dfrac{1 \text{ lb}}{8 \text{ servings}} \times \dfrac{1 \text{ box}}{10 \text{ lb}} = \dfrac{? \text{ boxes}}{\text{party}}$

4. $\dfrac{725 \times 2 \text{ boxes}}{8 \times 10 \text{ party}} = 18.125$, or about $19 \dfrac{\text{boxes}}{\text{party}}$

Always round up if the final answer is some kind of food.

▓▓▓▓▓ **EXAMPLE**

You are in charge of the concession stands at a football stadium. How much mustard do you need on hand? You will have to make some assumptions and remember a few facts:

Assumption #1	Past experience tells you that at a game like this, each person will consume an average of ½ hot dog.
Assumption #2	People usually put about 1 Tbsp of mustard on a hot dog.
Fact #1	There will be 75,000 fans and 500 workers at the game.
Fact #2	The only thing on the concession stand menu that requires mustard is hot dogs.
Fact #3	Mustard comes 4 gal/case.

Solution

1. "People at the game" will be the beginning label.
2. "Cases for the game" is the label on the answer.
3. $\dfrac{75,000 \text{ people}}{\text{game}} \times \dfrac{0.5 \text{ hot dogs}}{\text{person}} \times \dfrac{1 \text{ Tbsp}}{1 \text{ hotdog}} \times \dfrac{1 \text{ cup}}{16 \text{ Tbsp}} \times \dfrac{1 \text{ qt}}{4 \text{ cup}} \times \dfrac{1 \text{ gal}}{4 \text{ qt}} \times \dfrac{1 \text{ case}}{4 \text{ gal}}$

   $= ? \dfrac{\text{cases}}{\text{game}}$

4. $\dfrac{75,000 \times .5 \text{ cases}}{16 \times 4 \times 4 \times 4 \text{ game}} = 36.621$, or about $37 \dfrac{\text{cases}}{\text{game}}$

▇▇▇▇▇▇ **EXAMPLE**

How many tanks of post-mix soda will you need to feed 525 people 8 oz each? Post mix is mixed 4.75:1 water to syrup.

1. The label on the initial quantity is "people in the party."
2. The label in the answer should be "tanks per party."
3. $\dfrac{525 \text{ people}}{\text{party}} \times \dfrac{8 \text{ oz}}{\text{person}} \times \dfrac{1 \text{ gal soda}}{128 \text{ oz}} \times \dfrac{1 \text{ gal syrup}}{5.75 \text{ gal soda}} \times \dfrac{1 \text{ tank}}{5 \text{ gal syrup}} = ? \dfrac{\text{tank}}{\text{party}}$

4. $\dfrac{525 \times 8 \text{ tanks}}{128 \times 5.75 \times 5 \text{ party}} = 1.141$, or about $2 \dfrac{\text{tanks}}{\text{party}}$

   When converting any quantity containing a concentrate, remember that *both parts* of the water-to-syrup ratio are used. The ratio in this example is 4.75:1, but since both parts will be combined to make the soda there will be 5.75, not 4.75, parts of soda for every part of syrup. This same logic holds for any problem involving a concentrate.

▇▇▇▇▇▇ **EXAMPLE**

How many meters in 15 miles?

Solution

1. Begin with miles.
2. End with meters.
3. $15 \text{ mi.} \times \dfrac{5{,}280 \text{ ft.}}{1 \text{ mi.}} \times \dfrac{12 \text{ in.}}{1 \text{ ft.}} \times \dfrac{1 \text{ m}}{39.37 \text{ in.}} = ? \text{ m}$

4. $\dfrac{15 \times 5{,}280 \times 12 \text{ m}}{39.37} = 24{,}140.208 \text{ m}$

▇▇▇▇▇▇ **EXAMPLE**

How many #16 scoops are there in a gallon?

Solution

1. Begin with gallons.
2. End with #16 scoops.
3. $1 \text{ gal} \times \dfrac{4 \text{ qt}}{1 \text{ gal}} \times \dfrac{16 \text{ #16 scoops}}{1 \text{ qt}} = ? \text{ #16 scoops}$

4. $4 \times 16 \text{ (#16 scoops)} = 64 \text{ (#16 scoops)}$

EXAMPLE

How many gallons are there in 2,417 ml?

Solution

1. Begin with milliliters.
2. End with gallons.
3.
$$2{,}417 \text{ ml} \times \frac{1 \text{ L}}{1{,}000 \text{ ml}} \times \frac{1 \text{ qt}}{0.947 \text{ L}} \times \frac{1 \text{ gal}}{4 \text{ qt}} = ? \text{ gal}$$

4.
$$\frac{2{,}417 \text{ gal}}{1{,}000 \times 0.947 \times 4} = 0.638 \text{ gal}$$

Problems

Some units of conversion are more accurate than others, so only use the ones given in this chapter so that your answers will match those in the back of the book.

1. How many teaspoons in a cup?

2. How many inches in 3 yards?

3. How many cups in 15 gal?

4. How many #60 scoops in 2 cups?

5. How many people can be fed 8 oz of soup from 3 46-oz cans of mushroom soup concentrate (mixed 1:1 with water)?

6. How many quarts of orange juice concentrate will it take to give 6 oz each to 320 people (mixed 3:1 water to concentrate)?

7. How many #8 scoops are in 2 L?

8. How many milliliters are in 14 Tbsp?

9. How much raw corned beef brisket will you need if you wish to give 317 people 6 oz of cooked brisket each? Figure that raw corned beef brisket will shrink abou 50% during the cooking and trimming process.

10. How many kilometers in a mile?

11. How many people will 13 cases of peach halves feed, if there are 6 #10 cans in a case and each can contains 24 servings?

12. If a recipe uses 10 lb of ground beef to make 20 servings of meat loaf, how much ground beef will be needed to feed 340 people?

13. If you plan to serve 1½ oz of potato chips to each guest, how many 3-lb cases of bulk chips will it take to feed 75 people?

14. How many ounces in a 4-L jug of salad oil?

15. How many cases of lettuce will you need to make salads for 535 people, if you usually get about 85 salads from a case of 24-head iceberg lettuce?

16. Will 850 tsp of soy sauce fit into a gallon jug?

17. How many 2-kg wheels of brie cheese will you need to buy if you need 88 oz of cheese?

18. If beef patties come in 10-lb boxes, how many boxes of 5/1 patties will it take to feed 110 people one and one half burgers each?

19. How many #10 cans of catsup will be needed for the above party if each hamburger takes 15 ml of catsup and a #10 can holds 103.7 fluid oz?

20. How many pounds of dry coffee will you need if 13 oz of dry coffee makes 3 gal of brewed coffee and you plan to feed 300 people 2 6-oz cups of coffee each?

Glossary

AP   as purchased. Unrefined food as it exists at receiving.

AS   as served. The state of refinement needed at service. Total yield after cooking and processing.

AS/AP formula

$$AP = \frac{AS \times 100}{100 - W}$$

Bid order sheet   an order sheet that allows the purchaser to determine the cost of expensive products before they are purchased.

Bill of fare   the unadorned list of foods that the foodservice offers to the guest.

Build-to   another term for the word *par*. The term is to serve as a reminder that par is the maximum that is purchased, since stock on hand is always deducted from expected needs before any commodity is ordered.

Case size   the number of items contained in a case.

Customer count   the number of people served in a foodservice over a particular time period.

Cycle menu   A collection of menus that change from day to day, but repeat themselves when the last one has been used; items are offered in the same combinations when the cycle is repeated.

Daily usage par   the maximum amount of a product considered for use for a single day of service. An estimate of daily usage.

EP   edible portion. The amount of food the customer is expected to eat. The state of refinement allowing for complete consumption.

Equal cycle   a cycle containing as many menus as the days it is expected to cover.

Food production sheet   a form used by management to inform the production staff of the food they need to produce. Can also be used in any menu situation as a history-gathering tool for food removed from the kitchen.

Ingredient amount   the amount of an ingredient that the recipe specifies should be used to complete the recipe.

Inventory   dollar value of supplies on hand. When used with low-level par forecasting, the amount of a commodity in-house on order day.

Long cycle   a cycle containing more menus than the number of days it is designed to cover.

Low-level par the minimum amount of a commodity needed to last from one food delivery day to another.

Menu scatter sheet a form used to record food sold in the dining room. A history-gathering tool assembled from guest checks or a POS machine.

Miscellaneous order sheet an order sheet that enables the purchasing agent to buy items that are not purchased every ordering period.

Mise en place prepreparation.

Order sheet a form that organized, completed orders may be recorded on for the purpose of call-in.

Par an estimate of the quantity required for use over a specific time period.

Par order sheet an order sheet best suited to ordering the same items time after time.

Piece yield the number of AS servings that a business expects to get out of an AP market form.

Portion size (S) the serving size offered to each guest.

Product code (PC) the purveyor's code number representing a particular market form.

Recipe factor the number of times a recipe, or a baker's formula, should be increased or decreased to provide enough food to serve the expected number of customers.

Sales menu a menu that offers the same selections day after day; often called a static menu.

Special event menu a menu, usually used by a caterer, that is designed for a particular function and may never be used again.

Standardized recipe a recipe that has been tested by the business and found predictable in flavor, texture, appearance, and yield.

Unit of conversion (UOC) an expression having a value of one which allows for the conversion of one label on a quantity to another label.

Usable inventory used with a daily usage par to denote the amount of a commodity estimated to still be available for use when the newly ordered food is to be used.

Usable units the most common units used to describe the size of a commodity in the marketplace.

Usage ratio the amount that the average, individual guest has historically consumed; a useful forecasting tool for a cycle menu situation.

W waste. The waste incurred to bring the food to the AS or EP state of refinement.

W% waste percentage: $(W/AP) \times 100$.

Yield analysis factor (YAF) A labelless index designed to identify the waste/yield factors associated with a specific market form.

Answers to Odd-Numbered Problems

Chapter 4

1. $\dfrac{35 \text{ lb} \times 100}{100 - 37} = 55.556 \text{ lb, or about 56 lb AP}$

3. $175 \text{ people} \times \dfrac{4.5 \text{ oz}}{\text{person}} \times \dfrac{1 \text{ lb}}{16 \text{ oz}} = 49.219 \text{ lb AS}$

$\dfrac{49.219 \text{ lb} \times 100}{100 - 26} = 66.512 \text{ lb, or about 67 lb AP}$

5. 78 lb AP – 70 lb AS = 8 lb W

$\dfrac{8 \text{ lb}}{78 \text{ lb}} = 10.3\% \text{ W}$

7. $55 \text{ people} \times \dfrac{7 \text{ oz}}{\text{person}} \times \dfrac{1 \text{ lb}}{16 \text{ oz}} = 24.063 \text{ lb AS}$

$\dfrac{24.063 \text{ lb} \times 100}{100 - 46} = 44.561 \text{ lb, or about 50 lb AP round}$

9. $18 \text{ people} \times \dfrac{7 \text{ oz}}{\text{person}} \times \dfrac{1 \text{ lb}}{16 \text{ oz}} = 7.875 \text{ lb AS needed}$

Raw breast yield: 13 lb – (13 lb × 0.37) = 8.190 lb AS
Cooked breast yield: 13 lb – (13 lb × 0.015) = 12.805 lb AS
Either one will do.

11. Mashed potatoes. M&M's.

13. $\dfrac{13 \text{ lb AS}}{\text{recipe}} \times \dfrac{5 \text{ recipes}}{\text{party}} = \dfrac{65 \text{ lb AS}}{\text{party}}$

$\dfrac{65 \text{ lb} \times 100}{100 - 13} = 74.713 \text{ lb, or about 75 lb AP}$

15. $20 \text{ gal} \times \dfrac{8 \text{ pt}}{1 \text{ gal}} \times \dfrac{1 \text{ lb}}{1 \text{ pt}} = 160 \text{ lb AS}$

$$\frac{160 \text{ lb} \times 100}{100 - 52} = 333.333 \text{ lb AP}$$

$$333.333 \text{ lb} \times \frac{1 \text{ case}}{45 \text{ lb}} = 7.407, \text{ or about 8 cases}$$

17. 48 lb AS needed − 35 lb AS on hand = 13 lb AS yet to purchase

$$\frac{13 \text{ lb} \times 100}{100 - 29} = 18.310 \text{ lb, or about 19 lb AP}$$

19.
$$4 \text{ cases} \times \frac{12 \text{ bottles}}{1 \text{ case}} \times \frac{0.2 \text{ gal}}{\text{bottle}} \times \frac{8 \text{ pt}}{1 \text{ gal}} \times \frac{1 \text{ lb}}{1 \text{ pt}} = 76.8 \text{ lb AS}$$

$$\frac{76.8 \text{ lb} \times 100}{100 - 47} = 144.906 \text{ lb AP}$$

$$144.906 \text{ lb} \times \frac{1 \text{ case}}{28 \text{ lb}} = 5.175, \text{ or about 6 cases}$$

Chapter 5

1. Sunday breakfast: The average is 9, so you could safely expect to feed about 10 people.
3. Wednesday dinner: The average is 891. Each previous count is not too far off of that, so your cushion can be small. Figure on feeding about 895.
5. Friday dinner: The average is 497. Plan on feeding an even 500.

Chapter 6

1. White bread:

   28 + 26 + 46 + 21 + 13 = 134 sandwiches

   $$134 \text{ sandwiches} \times \frac{2 \text{ slices}}{\text{sandwich}} = 268 \text{ slices}$$

   $$268 \text{ slices} \times \frac{1 \text{ loaf}}{22 \text{ slices}} = 12.182, \text{ or about 13 loaves}$$

3. Rye bread:

   37 + 15 + 64 + 43 + 56 = 215 sandwiches

   $$215 \text{ sandwiches} \times \frac{2 \text{ slices}}{\text{sandwich}} = 430 \text{ slices}$$

   $$430 \text{ slices} \times \frac{1 \text{ loaf}}{13 \text{ slices}} = 33.077, \text{ or about 34 loaves}$$

5. Onion rolls:

   42 + 26 + 31 + 32 + 48 = 179 sandwiches

   $$179 \text{ rolls} \times \frac{1 \text{ package}}{12 \text{ rolls}} = 14.917, \text{ or about 15 packages}$$

7. White bread order:

   $$\frac{13 \text{ loaves}}{\text{day}} \times \frac{3 \text{ days}}{\text{delivery}} = 39 \text{ loaves maximum}$$

   39 loaves − 5 loaves on hand = 34 loaves to order

9. Rye bread order:

$$\frac{33 \text{ loaves}}{\text{day}} \times \frac{3 \text{ days}}{\text{delivery}} = 99 \text{ loaves maximum}$$

99 loaves − 0 loaves on hand = 99 loaves to order

11. Onion roll order

$$\frac{15 \text{ packages}}{\text{day}} \times \frac{3 \text{ days}}{\text{delivery}} = 45 \text{ packages maximum}$$

45 packages − 0 packages on hand = 45 packages to order

Chapter 7

Menu Item	Forecasted Customer Count	Usage Ratio	Food Forecast
Tuesday Week 1	875		
F F chicken		0.235 hd/C	206 head
Sweet & sour pork		0.331 S/C	290 S
Ham & cheese sandwich		0.520 S/C	455 sand
Wednesday Week 1	850		
Roast beef		0.261 lb AP/C	222 lb AP
Chicken pot pie		0.163 S/C	139 S
Stuffed pepper		0.106 S/C	91 S
Thursday Week 1	895		
Pork chops		0.889 ea/C	796 S
Arroz con pollo		0.111 S/C	100 S
Meat loaf		0.333 S/C	298 S
Friday Week 1	640		
Spaghetti & meat sauce		0.628 S/C	402 S
Turkey & dressing		0.076 lb AP/C	49 lb AP
Corned beef & cabbage		0.063 lb AP/C	41 lb AP
Saturday Week 1	325		
Hamburger		1.062 S/C	346 S
F F clams		0.004 bx/C	2 boxes
Pepper steak		0.089 S/C	29 S
Sunday Week 1	435		
Baked salmon		0.128 lb AP/C	56 lb AP
Beef stroganoff		0.297 S/C	130 S
Sloppy Joe		0.099 S/C	43 S
Monday Week 1	845		
Pizza		0.253 pie/C	214 14″
Baked ham		0.042 lb AP/C	36 lb AP
Chicken chow mein		0.169 S/C	143 S

Chapter 8

1. *Customer*   *Portion*
      Count   *Size*

$$\frac{413 \text{ people}}{\text{reception}} \times \frac{6 \text{ shrimp}}{\text{person}} \times \frac{1 \text{ lb}}{23 \text{ shrimp}} = 107.7 \text{ lb, or about 108 lb}$$

for the party

3. *Customer*   *Portion*
      Count   *Size*

$$\frac{413 \text{ people}}{\text{reception}} \times \frac{1 \text{ potato}}{\text{person}} \times \frac{1 \text{ case}}{80 \text{ potatoes}} = 5.163 \text{ cases, or about 6 cases}$$

for the reception

5. *Customer*   *Portion*
      Count   *Size*

$$\frac{413 \text{ people}}{\text{reception}} \times \frac{0.5 \text{ head}}{\text{person}} = 206.5 \text{ head, or about 207 heads}$$

Chapter 9

1. $80 \text{ people} \times \dfrac{1 \text{ recipe}}{15 \text{ people}} = 5.333, \text{ or a recipe factor of } 5.5$

$5.5 \text{ recipes} \times \dfrac{2 \text{ lb}}{\text{recipe}} = 11 \text{ lb snow peas}$

3. $130 \text{ people} \times \dfrac{1 \text{ recipe}}{15 \text{ people}} = 8.667, \text{ or a recipe factor of } 9$

$9 \text{ recipes} \times \dfrac{10 \text{ oz}}{\text{recipe}} \times \dfrac{1 \text{ lb}}{16 \text{ oz}} = 5.625, \text{ or about 5 lb 10 oz}$

5. $45 \text{ people} \times \dfrac{1 \text{ recipe}}{15 \text{ people}} = \text{ a recipe factor of } 3$

$3 \text{ recipes} \times \dfrac{1.5 \text{ lb}}{\text{recipe}} = 4.5 \text{ lb of buds AS}$

$\text{AP} = \dfrac{4.5 \times 100}{100 - 62} = 11.842, \text{ or about 12 lb AP}$

Chapter 10

1. $340 \text{ people} \times \dfrac{1 \text{ inside}}{55 \text{ people}} = 6.182, \text{ or about 6.5 insides}$

3. $480 \text{ people} \times \dfrac{1 \text{ case}}{95 \text{ people}} = 5.053, \text{ or about 5 cases and 2 heads}$

5. $340 \text{ people} \times \dfrac{1 \text{ gal}}{100 \text{ people}} = 3.4, \text{ or about 3.5 gal}$

Chapter 11

1. Inside round: 1.426

3. Raw, bone-in turkey breast: 1.816

5. BRT pork loin: 1.695

7. Raw, whole corned beef brisket: 2.000

9. Cooked, boneless ham: 1.123

11. Roast beef:

   a. Best buy:
   Inside: $1.426 \times \$2.86 = \$4.08/\text{AS lb}$
   Outside: $1.570 \times \$2.63 = \$4.13/\text{AS lb}$
   Inside is the best buy of the week.

   b.
   $$380 \text{ people} \times \frac{6 \text{ oz}}{\text{person}} \times \frac{1 \text{ lb}}{16 \text{ oz}} = 142.5 \text{ lb AS}$$

   $142.5 \text{ lb AS} \times 1.426 = 203.205$, or 204 lb AP inside

   c.
   $$\text{AP cost} = 204 \text{ lb AP} \times \frac{\$2.86}{\text{lb AP}} = \$583.44$$

13. Roast beef:

   a. Inside round is still the best buy.

   b.
   $$310 \text{ people} \times \frac{6 \text{ oz}}{\text{person}} \times \frac{1 \text{ lb}}{16 \text{ oz}} = 116.25 \text{ lb AS}$$

   $116.25 \text{ lb AS} \times 1.426 = 165.773$, or 166 lb AP inside

   c.
   $$\text{AP cost} = 166 \text{ lb AP} \times \frac{\$2.86}{\text{lb AP}} = \$474.76$$

15. Baked ham:

   a. Best buy:
   Ckd. bnls. ham: $1.123 \times \$2.08 = \$2.34/\text{AS lb}$
   Unckd. B.I. ham: $1.640 \times \$1.33 = \$2.18/\text{AS lb}$
   Uncooked bone-in ham is the best buy this week.

   b.
   $$250 \text{ people} \times \frac{7 \text{ oz}}{\text{person}} \times \frac{1 \text{ lb}}{16 \text{ oz}} = 109.375 \text{ lb AS}$$

   $109.375 \text{ lb} \times 1.640 = 179.375$, or about 180 lb AP

   c.
   $$\text{AP cost} = 180 \text{ lb AP} \times \frac{\$1.33}{\text{lb AP}} = \$239.40$$

Chapter 13

1. Round of beef by the AP lb.

   a. Best buy:
   Inside: $1.426 \times \$2.94 = \$4.19/\text{lb AS}$
   Outside: $1.570 \times \$2.76 = \$4.33/\text{lb AS}$
   Inside round is the best buy for this order period.

b. AS needs:

Italian beef:
    DU par × days
    18 lb AS/day × 3 days = 54 lb AS

Wed. roast beef:
    Usage ratio × FCC
    0.246 lb/C × 430 C = 105.78, or 106 lb AS

Fri. BBQ beef:
    Usage ratio × FCC
    0.106 lb AS/C × 435 C = 46.11, or 47 lb AS

Mon. Sauerbraten:
    remember mise en place
    Usage ratio × FCC
    0.216 lb AS/C × 415 C = 89.64, or 90 lb AS

Total inside round needs:
    54 lb AS + 106 lb AS + 47 lb AS + 90 lb AS = 297 lb AS

c. AP needs: AS amount × YAF
    297 lb × 1.426 = 423.522, or 424 lb AP

d. AP order: AP needs − Usable inventory
    424 lb AP − 7 lb AP = 417 lb AP
Call in an order for 417 lb of AP inside round.

3. Sliced American cheese by the 3-lb block:

a. Need: LL par

b. Order: LL par − inventory
    (4 3-lb blk) − (1 3-lb blk) = 3 3-lb blk
Call in an order for 3 3-lb blocks of sliced American cheese.

5. Bulk hamburger by the 10-lb bag:

a. AS needs:

Thu. for spaghetti sc.:
UR × FCC
0.181 S/C × 450 C = 81.45, or 82 S
Servings needed ÷ Recipe yield = Recipe factor
$$82 \text{ S} \times \frac{1 \text{ recipe}}{75 \text{ S}} = 1.5 \text{ recipes}$$
Remember to round up to next ½ recipe to have your answers come out like the ones here.
Recipe fac. × ingred. amt. = Tot. ingred. wt.
$$1.5 \text{ recipes} \times \frac{10 \text{ lb}}{\text{recipe}} = 15 \text{ lb AP}$$

Fri. Chopped steak:
UR × FCC
0.316 S/C × 435 C = 137.46, or 138 S
Servings needed ÷ Recipe yield = Recipe factor
$$138 \text{ S} \times \frac{1 \text{ recipe}}{30 \text{ S}} = 4.6, \text{ rounded to 5 rec.}$$
Recipe fac. × ingred. amt. = Tot. ingred. wt.
$$5 \text{ recipes} \times \frac{10 \text{ lb}}{\text{recipe}} = 50 \text{ lb AP}$$

Total AP needs:
    15 lb + 50 lb = 65 lb AP

b. Order: AP needs − usable inventory

65 lb AP – 10 lb AP = 55 lb AP
Call in an order for 60 lb of AP ground beef because it comes in 10-lb bags.

7. Shoestring french fries by the 27-lb case.

a. Need: LL par

b. Order: par – inventory
4 cases – 2 cases = 2 cases
Call in an order for 2 cases of fries.

9. Hot dogs, all beef, 8/1, by the 10-lb box:

a. Need: DU par × days
8 lb AP/day × 3 days = 24 lb AP

b. Order: AP needs – usable inventory
24 lb AP – 4 lb AP = 20 lb AP
Call in an order for 2 boxes of hot dogs.

11. PSMO tenderloin by the AP lb:

a. Need:
Wed. party:
CC × portion size, converted to usable units

$$36 \text{ people} \times \frac{6 \text{ oz}}{\text{person}} \times \frac{1 \text{ lb}}{16 \text{ oz}} = 13.5, \text{ or } 14 \text{ lb AP}$$

b. Order: AP needs – usable inventory
14 lb AP – 0 lb AP = 14 lb AP
Call in an order for 14 lb of AP PSMO tenderloin.

13. 2½-lb chicken quarters by the head:

a. Need:
Thu. fried chicken:
UR × FCC
0.183 hd./C × 450 C = 82.35, or 83 hd.

b. Order: AP needs – usable inventory
83 hd. – 0 hd. = 83 hd.
Call in an order for 83 head of 2½-lb chix quarters.

15. Hamburger buns by the dozen:

a. Need: DU par × days
9 dozen/day × 3 days = 27 dozen

b. Order: Need – usable inventory
27 dozen – 0 dozen = 27 dozen
Call in an order for 27 packages of hamburger buns.

17. Carrots by the 50-lb sack:

a. Need: LL par

b. Order: LL par – inventory
50 lb – 10 lb = 40 lb
Call in an order for 1 50-lb sack of carrots.

19. Lettuce by the 24-head case:

a. Need: LL par
Order: LL par – inventory
3 cases – 2 cases = 1 case
Call in an order for 1 case of 24-head iceberg lettuce.

Appendix

1. $1 \text{ cup} \times \dfrac{16 \text{ Tbsp}}{1 \text{ cup}} \times \dfrac{3 \text{ tsp}}{1 \text{ Tbsp}} = 48 \text{ tsp}$

3. $15 \text{ gal} \times \dfrac{4 \text{ qt}}{1 \text{ gal}} \times \dfrac{2 \text{ pt}}{1 \text{ qt}} \times \dfrac{2 \text{ cups}}{1 \text{ pt}} = 240 \text{ cups}$

5. $3 \text{ cans} \times \dfrac{46 \text{ oz concentrate}}{1 \text{ can}} \times \dfrac{2 \text{ oz soup}}{1 \text{ oz con.}} \times \dfrac{1 \text{ person}}{8 \text{ oz soup}}$
$= 34.5$, or about 34 people

7. $2 \text{ L} \times \dfrac{1 \text{ qt}}{0.947 \text{ L}} \times \dfrac{8 \text{ (\#8 scoops)}}{1 \text{ qt}} = 16.895 \text{ \#8 scoops}$

9. $\dfrac{317 \text{ people}}{\text{party}} \times \dfrac{6 \text{ oz ckd.}}{\text{person}} \times \dfrac{2 \text{ oz raw}}{1 \text{ oz ckd.}} \times \dfrac{1 \text{ lb}}{16 \text{ oz}} = 237.75$, or
about 238 lb raw C. B. B.

11. $13 \text{ cases} \times \dfrac{6 \text{ cans}}{1 \text{ case}} \times \dfrac{24 \text{ children}}{1 \text{ can}} = 1872 \text{ children}$

13. $\dfrac{75 \text{ people}}{\text{party}} \times \dfrac{1.5 \text{ oz}}{\text{person}} \times \dfrac{1 \text{ lb}}{16 \text{ oz}} \times \dfrac{1 \text{ case}}{3 \text{ lb}} = 2.344$, or about 3 cases to feed the
party

15. $\dfrac{535 \text{ people}}{\text{party}} \times \dfrac{1 \text{ case}}{85 \text{ people}} = 6.294$, or about 7 cases

17. $88 \text{ oz} \times \dfrac{1 \text{ lb}}{16 \text{ oz}} \times \dfrac{1 \text{ kg}}{2.2 \text{ lb}} \times \dfrac{1 \text{ wheel}}{2 \text{ kg}} = 1.25$, or about 2 wheels

19. $\dfrac{110 \text{ people}}{\text{party}} \times \dfrac{1.5 \text{ burgers}}{\text{person}} \times \dfrac{15 \text{ ml}}{1 \text{ burger}} \times \dfrac{1 \text{ L}}{1000 \text{ ml}} \times \dfrac{1 \text{ qt}}{0.947 \text{ L}} \times \dfrac{32 \text{ oz}}{1 \text{ qt}}$
$\times \dfrac{1 \text{ \#10 can}}{103.7 \text{ oz}} = 0.806$, or about 1 #10 can for this party

Tear-Out Forms

Menu Scatter Sheet

Week Ending / /

Menu Item	Guest Check Sales Tally							Total Sold	×	Selling Price	=	Menu Item Revenue Contribution	÷	Total Net Sales	=	Percent Contribution to Sales
	M	T	W	T	F	S	S									
									×		=		÷		=	
									×		=		÷		=	
									×		=		÷		=	
									×		=		÷		=	
									×		=		÷		=	
									×		=		÷		=	
									×		=		÷		=	
									×		=		÷		=	
									×		=		÷		=	
									×		=		÷		=	
									×		=		÷		=	
									×		=		÷		=	
									×		=		÷		=	
									×		=		÷		=	
									×		=		÷		=	

Customer Count:

Comments:

155

Food Production Sheet   Day: _____   Date _____ / _____ / _____

Customer Count:					
Menu Item	Portion Size	Amount to Prepare	Amount Actually Prepared	Amount Left Over or CC RO or Time RO	Amount Used

Comments:

Par Order Sheet

Food Category:	Purveyor:		Telephone Number: _ _ - _ _

Item & Description	Low-level Par	Delivery Dates					
PC: _____							
PC: _____							
PC: _____							
PC: _____							
PC: _____							
PC: _____							
PC: _____							
PC: _____							
PC: _____							
PC: _____							
PC: _____							
PC: _____							
PC: _____							
PC: _____							
PC: _____							
PC: _____							
PC: _____							
PC: _____							
PC: _____							
PC: _____							
PC: _____							
PC: _____							
PC: _____							
PC: _____							
PC: _____							
PC: _____							
PC: _____							
PC: _____							
PC: _____							

Bid Order Sheet

Delivery Date: / /		Purveyor #1		Purveyor #2		Purveyor #3	
Item & Description	Order	Bid	Cost	Bid	Cost	Bid	Cost
Individual Invoice Total:							

Miscellaneous Order Sheet

Delivery Date: / /		Purveyor:	Telephone Number: - -
Product Code	Order	Item & Description	

Index

ISBN 0-02-422101-5

9 780024 221018